THE CREATIVE VIRUS

Michael Joseph

Table of Contents

To my friend Kevin Ryan
Who always encouraged me to
chase my dreams
and live my faith.
R.I.P.

Introduction

I should warn you … you are about to read a book written by a person who doesn't enjoy reading books.

WAIT, don't quit now please!

I promise this book will contain:

Clichés with uniqueness.

Things you've seen but now through new eyes.

Stories that are old but full of life.

Lessons learned and learned again.

People, places, and things for that person, stuck in a place, because of a thing.

And most importantly, hope for your heart.

Thank you for staying. On to chapter one!

Chapter 1
The Epiphany Moments

Hi, my name is Michael Joseph. I have spent my entire life chasing fame and fortune. I've tried to achieve acclaim in one area of the entertainment world or another. In that pursuit, I've given up or even lost SO many things. I've lost friends, girlfriends, jobs, a home, financial stability, not to mention both my physical and mental health. On more than one occasion, I have walked away from the opportunity to make "real money." My pursuit of fame and fortune has led me down a path far from the norm. That alternate course allowed me to meet some amazing people and took me to places I could never have gone if I chose the "normal" route.

For me to say I should have taken another path would be to go against my faith and how I know life works.
Many times, I tried to plan things out.
I've tried to take the more traveled road, or to just be like everyone else. I tried to work a "respectable" job and be like … whoever "everyone else" is trying to be. It didn't matter what direction I headed; I still found myself off the beaten path yet on a direct compass heading towards an unknown future. When I tried to divert and take a shortcut or the scenic route, I just ended up where I would have been if I had kept moving forward. I was never lost, but I did lose why I was headed that way in the first place.

There were plenty of times along that journey I may have felt either lost, like a failure, or both. Looking back, I see I was never off compass. Lost, never, but I was certainly blind to my surroundings at different moments in time. I was blind to little victories, blind to achievements or milestones that should have been celebrated. I was blind to who was around me that truly cared. I was blind to people I pushed by to get to the goal. Moments in life that I should have stopped and remembered as cherished memories are now just throwback stories and pictures that gain a few social media clicks and likes.

Don't get me wrong, I regret nothing. I just wished I could have seen each moment for the real reason I was working so hard. To stop and see those moments up close and hands-on, not just pass them by on my way to the next destination. I hope I don't sound mournful about those moments. I know my life isn't over, and this very book is full of past events that I revisit with hopeful joy. So, take a few minutes with me as I look back at the exact point when this book came roaring to life. For now, I want to use the word *epiphany* to describe that moment or, more specifically, the two different moments that happened at almost the same time.

It was a typical day for the "new normal." About two-and-a-half weeks after the beginning of the COVID-19 "stay at home" order, around March 22nd, epiphanies happened April 10th. The first of the two moments I call the "why" and the second I call the "how." The "why" came to me like a tiny spark. Tiny only because it was overshadowed by me kicking myself for doubting the second, which was the "how." Try to stay with me because it happened so fast it's hard to describe them as two totally different yet significant inceptions.

In that moment, I found myself traveling through years and years of memories, each one a distinct step in that long journey. In every one of those memories, I saw the "why." The real reason I kept traveling down that path. How did I not see it for what it was, the real motivation that kept me going? Everything was in focus when I looked at the path in reverse. The "how" came next, and it was just as plain in hindsight. It was not only possible, but it was telling me every step of a journey that hadn't even begun yet. Before I get too deep talking about those moments, let me give you a little back story about Michael Joseph.

Believe it or not, my creativity started at an extremely young age. I don't remember this, but my mother told me when I was 5 years old. I asked her, "Why don't they have windows in the roofs of cars to let the sun in? "There is no way I had ever seen a sunroof at that point in life. It was way before most cars had them. It's a little strange but not surprising that I was already thinking creatively or at least had a great imagination. To some, *creative* and *imaginative* are two totally different things, but later in this book, I will take an in-depth look at the difference between creative, expressive, and imaginative.

Creativity was encouraged in my family. My mother owned an arts and crafts store for years. She was known for being quite a talented tole painter, not to mention SO many other arts and crafts. At her store, she taught classes and gave instructions to students from everywhere. If the internet was around back then, she would undoubtedly have an incredible following online with how-to videos or a Blog. My father was very talented as well. He was a woodworker, a gifted trumpeter, and a singer. With arts being a daily part of my life as a young person, I didn't see the limitations that life squeezed you with as you got older.

I just grabbed onto the creative handlebars and went forward as fast as I could go.

Throughout my life, I was exposed to and tackled just about every type of creativity there was in the world - drawing, painting, sculpting, writing, acting, and dancing. I put heart and soul into making music, making videos, vocal performing, DJing, and any other expressive opportunity that I thought could bring me fame. Throughout this book, I would like to take you on a tour of my creative journey. I know that most people may not relate to all areas I've worked in, but I hope that at least one of them resonates with you and your journey. Now let's get back to the "why" moment.

When the COVID-19 "stay at home" order started, I was a full-time DJ and a reporter for a company called Disc Jockey News. I spent at least three or more nights a week DJing at Clubs and Bars. The rest of my time I spent writing articles and making videos about new DJ products, DJ educational, and how-to DJ videos. I was either in front of people DJing or in front of the camera talking about DJing. When the stay-at-home order came down, all of that stopped.

This is where the first epiphany moment hit. I obviously wasn't performing to a crowd. There wasn't anyone; I lived alone. I wasn't making money anymore either. All venues for performance or avenues of income dried up instantly. This was pretty much the same for everyone in my industry. Yet each morning, I got up and kept working just like I did before the world came to a stop. I worked on scripts and articles, kept working on music, and practiced DJing. It was business as usual for me.

After a few weeks, I wondered why I kept getting up and going through this process each day? I'm not performing for anyone, and I'm not making any money. It was a complete absence of what I knew the path to "Fame and Fortune" to be. Yet there I was, still working hard every day. That's when it hit me ... It wasn't fame or any of the things that came along with fame. It wasn't fortune or anything that riches could buy. It was the act of being creative each day that I loved. It seems so pointless, yet like oxygen, I couldn't live without it.

Could all the struggles and choices to "make it" be rooted in something that pure? Was the act of being creative the fuel that made my fire burn? What about all the times I gave up tangible things for "exposure opportunities" to make it famous? Whoa ... how many things did I miss out on while chasing the illusion of bright lights and big money?

At that point, it was like everything fell away, and the only thing left standing was just my humble creativity greeting me like an old friend. It had been with me all along. It knew that everything else was smoke and mirrors, yet it let me believe in the illusion of fame and fortune so that I would keep spending time with it day after day. As everything cleared away, the only thing that was left was my old friend ... creativity.

The more I thought about this, the more I realized I could never chase it away, and I now knew I didn't want to. I still looked at each picture I drew or photo I edited with the same passion. I kept writing scripts and recording videos without skipping a beat. All that time, I was doing whatever I could to keep creating. Updating my website, working on my press kit. DJing online streaming sets alone in my studio. When most other people stopped everything, I was starting new projects. My brain's process of thinking, imagining, creating, and expressing was the "why."

Once I realized that creating is what I longed for, it actually took a lot of pressure off everything else. I didn't have to worry so much about the final product. Instead, I started to enjoy the process of creating. It really made things better by slowing down my mind. I worked on things not to just complete them but to enjoy creating. I know that sounds like that cliché "Life Is About The Journey, Not The Destination," but sometimes it can be both. It can be a rushed journey to get to a completed destination, or it could be a casual walk inside a creative bubble.

At that point, I realized I wasn't noticing as many things going on around me as I did before. I didn't care as much about what others were saying. It was like walking through a door and being in a whole new room with totally different lighting and a fresh breeze. So let me give you a peek at the surface of the creative mind.

My point of view is not everyone's when it comes to the creative mind. I know that the creative world is so much more complex than my words here. These are just generalized starting points to help you better accept and embrace the different parts of your creativity. I look at the creative world as having three different types of people: The Entertainer, The Artist and The Performer. From my point of view, they are separated by their motivation, yet any person can embody one, two, or all three of them at any given time.

The Entertainer would say to you, "Sit back in your chair. You are about to be entertained. "The Artist would say, "Get up out of your chair, come with me, I'm going to take you on a journey." And last, The Performer would say "Hey, look what I can do with a chair." The Entertainer wants to give part of themselves to the audience. The Artist wants to let out what is inside of their soul. The Performer wants to amaze anyone taking in what they are doing.

For the entertainer, the reward is how others react. They want to make the audience feel something. The artist wants to feel something in that act of letting out what is inside. The Performer feels most alive and full of purpose when the audience is moved by the act being performed. All three of them can be on the rollercoaster of life and see it totally differently. All three know they are not in control of the coaster, yet they ride for different reasons.

The Artist just loves going for a ride, no matter where it takes them or who is with them. The Entertainer loves the ride as long as they are helping others enjoy every twist and turn. The Performer, through whatever action, will make the ride bigger and better. The Artist, The Entertainer, and The Performer all know they are not in control of where the coaster goes, but to each one, every loop can be an uncharted journey from their creative point of view.

I know life is not like that for everyone. The average person completes a task and gets a reward. Do your job, get a paycheck. I understand everyone has to make a living. Everyone has responsibilities, but when you are deep in that creative moment, everything else fades away. To get lost in an endless bound of creativity is priceless. I don't care how much money you have; you can't buy that moment. I don't care how many classes you take; you can't learn that moment. It doesn't matter the endless resources or support you have; you can't manufacture that moment. You can only give that moment to yourself. When you can just sit surrounded by what your mind creates, then and only then will you understand why it is so priceless.

I'm not saying that other things in life aren't valuable, but if you feel you are one of the two above-mentioned people and realize that creativity is your driving force. You see it as your foundation, your root system; you will prioritize creativity to be first amongst all the other things in the work process.

It is a power source with the best return. You know you have to make money; you know you need to get the job done but tapping into the creative process as your fuel makes things a lot less stressful, not to mention it removes the fear of failing. There is no failure in being creative. Even if you miss the mark, you still created something.

The whole epiphany was still very much on my mind when the "how" spoke up and turned that little spark into a full-blown fire. I was watching a show on TV called "Making It." It is a reality/game show about people who make things with their hands. Many are crafters like my mother was. Others were woodworkers like my father was. Each week they are given different themed tasks to complete. These tasks are then judged by two experts in the field.

It amazed me at how the different contestants didn't seem like they were competing with each other. When one would finish their project, they would help another competitor finish theirs. It was just people being creative together. I was so moved by this show because it spoke to the creative person inside me. My mind started to flood with all the different areas I have been creative in throughout my life. I remembered how the area of writing helped with making videos. I remembered how photography class helped with stage performances. So, I started writing down notes about each area and the creative elements that built them. Before I knew it, I had pages and pages of things written down. That was the "how." I can turn the notes into a book to help others find their creative spark.

It doesn't matter if you want to make your home feel more welcoming or if you need to solve international-level problems. You can use creativity to fix a leaky sink or creatively use duct tape and an old sock to keep the Apollo 13 astronauts alive. All reasons for creativity should be embraced. It doesn't matter if it's used to escape something mentally, to energize your soul, or just to enjoy its process; creativity can be a potent cure for what ails you.

When life paused during the lockdown, I got to look at my entire life and see that being creative was not just something I did; it was inside me like a virus my whole life. Keep in mind a virus is not a living thing like bacteria. It is more like a set of instructions (a small collection of genetic code) that get put into a living cell, telling that cell to make copies of itself with the instructions enclosed. They can't replicate themselves without being inside a cell; they need the cell. Those instructions then become part of our DNA. So, when we catch the creative virus, it becomes a part of us forever. Viruses aren't like bacteria; you can't use antibiotics to kill them. You can only use antiviral medication to keep the virus from leaving one cell and infecting others or vaccines to trigger the body's immune system into creating antibodies against it. Think of the creative virus as a good set of instructions that cause you to want to be creative. The only way to keep that virus at bay (stop the endless drive to be creative) is to be creative. Thus, my continual need to seek opportunities to create. I can't turn it off; I can only reduce the severe need to be creative … by being creative.

As I transition to other chapters in this book, I will cover my creative process in many areas. Some you will relate to quickly, while others will seem like total babble. I want you to think about your life and think about what you create. I want you to think about how you use creativity to solve everyday tasks. Remember, creativity isn't just about artwork. It can be about creatively solving a problem like what to make for dinner or how to change the recipe for a picky eater. You can use it to figure out why the wiring system on your lawn mower isn't working. You may need to create room in your budget to take your family on vacation or to decorate your own house with a unique touch that no one else has.

Whatever form your creativity takes, let go of your surroundings and immerse yourself in that process. Keep telling yourself there is no wrong outcome as long as the journey is pure. Whatever you create may not be what's in your mind, but that doesn't mean that it's wrong. If something turns out different from what you saw in your imagination, remember, other people can't see how different it is from what was in your head. To them, it might be beautiful and perfect just the way it is. Each creation has its own worth. That's not only true with art but also with you as a person. No matter what you think, you are not a mistake, and you are not broken. If you feel you are broken, keep this in mind; even a broken crayon can create a beautiful picture.

Chapter 2
An Origin Story

Prior to the digital age, my life, like most other creative people, was full of little pieces of paper. The content of those little pieces of paper could be just about anything. It might be song lyrics, a melody line, or just a concept title for a song. They could be poems, a play, or just a picture I drew. Maybe a complete project of something I wanted to build or simple doodles to just get a thought out of my head. It was just things inside me that had to get out. Some of those things might be very long, complex projects, while others could be just a quote I thought of and wanted to remember for later. Whatever it was, I saved piles and piles of notes just in case that specific moment of inspiration was needed down the road.

Many people didn't understand this constant need to jot down ideas, but I accepted it as a normal part of my life, so much so that I couldn't imagine not doing that. I was blessed to have an atmosphere around me growing up that encouraged creativity. Art supplies were in abundance, both at home and at school. Not to mention that I grew up on a farm way out in the middle of nowhere, WAY before the internet, and no, we didn't get cable TV either. When I wasn't doing farm work, I had a lot of time on my hands to think, imagine and create.

For me, my favorite form of creativity was just a pencil or pen and paper. There was just something fun about sitting and drawing full landscapes, tiny cartoons, or even just stick figures in a flipbook. I don't know why, but I've always loved to draw. I was that typical artist that had several sketchbooks. You would be hard-pressed to find two drawings inside that had anything to do with each other. Mostly just sketches and doodles. It could be cartoons or beautiful scenery. I tended to be very polar like that when it came to styles of art. Sometimes the pictures were so serious and detailed, while others were pointless exaggerations of life around me. It's funny that my two favorite types of art to draw were opposites. One was the basic dance between dark and light using a pencil or ink pen; the other was warm, full-color drawings with pastel chalks or pencils.

Although I didn't know it then, I was using drawing as my escape to deal with life. I would draw these tiny little worlds. Some were full cities from the future with flying cars, rockets, and futuristic styled buildings influenced by the Jetsons or artwork from Popular Mechanics magazines from the 1960s. Other drawings would be just simple mountain tops, wide-open landscapes showing a scenic vastness empty of everything man-made and not a person in sight. Both were great places to let my mind escape to for hours. Nowadays, I tend to lean towards the mountains. Cities are a lot noisier in real life than they were in my drawings.

Pretty much every grade-schooler draws to some extent. Most kids back then drew a lot. As I got older, I believe that art helped me as a non-typical young person connect with the world around me. Conversations could be easily started by someone else asking, "What have you been drawing lately?" Conversely, if you were face down on a desk drawing, most people won't interrupt. Not having to communicate because I was drawing solved a lot of problems for the time being. On paper, I could easily express how I felt without those feelings affecting anyone around me. Anger, fear, excitement, joy, or any other emotion could be fully expressed without saying a single word to another human. You will see this is a recurring theme in my life. I'm not a "people person," but I have great people skills that sometimes come at a considerable self-cost.

When I say, "I'm not a people person," people who don't really know me think there is a punchline coming. It may not seem like it with my career choice, but I'm really not. Some people get together with their friends or loved ones to have fun and recharge their batteries. That is not me. Sometimes just answering back a text can be draining on my personal battery. Keep in mind there is a big difference between shyness and introversion. I'm not shy, I'm not even sure I'm introverted, but like many artists, I value time alone more than I do time with others. It's nothing against people in general; it's just sometimes it's not worth the gamble of socializing when compared to how draining it is in the end.

I didn't enjoy high school much, but I think that is where my creativity shifted into high gear. The public high school I went to had every type of art class you could imagine. By the end of my senior year, I had taken every one the school offered. Drawing, painting, sculpting, photography, music classes, and the list goes on. Whatever they had to offer, I wanted to take. It was a wonderful exposure to such a diverse range of creative expressions. As I remember what those classes meant to me, it leaves me speechless watching schools drop the arts to fund other "activities." I can't imagine a sea of artists that never got to find their expressive outlet because of budget cuts that ended up going to other school events where people would pay to watch.

Even though I was able to pursue so many specific art forms, high school was also where I started to mix mediums. For those who don't know, mixing mediums would be if a painter used something other than paint in their picture. It's kinda frowned upon using a pen to define lines in a painting. I didn't see what the big deal was. After all, I wasn't trying to get my art in a museum or sell it; I was just creating a picture. As technology and the internet give artists the chance to share their creation with the world, I find Mixed Media artists everywhere. That style of art is not only accepted but is appreciated.

As I went through each class, I not only learned that type of art but also how to tell a story through pictures. I think that's why I gravitated towards it, I'm a visual thinker. I see the world in a combination of images. If you asked me to create something, all I would do is go into a giant room in my mind and just start pulling out pictures of stuff I've previously seen. Most of them may have nothing to do with what you ask to be created. I just take a little piece of this one and a little of that one and put them together into one final product. That may sound difficult to you, but it is as easy to me as opening my eyes. Everything I need is already there. For me, coming up with new ideas or new concepts is like looking through a list of ingredients and mixing them into something new and awesome.

High school was also when I began playing music. At that time, it probably sounded more like random noise than music, but I started playing drums for my church's worship band and taking piano lessons in school. Of all the arts, playing music gave me the biggest challenge. The drums weren't too hard, but the piano took a LOT of work. Little did I know that in the future, things would soon start to click musically. There was a digital age of production and mixing coming about a decade down the road.

As many opportunities as I had in high school, college is where my creative path became a five-lane highway with lots of off and on-ramps. I continued to draw, but I tried out so many alternative forms of creativity. It's all a blur now, but I will do my best to point out many noteworthy stopping points along this tour for you.

I entered my freshman year of college as a communication major. I wanted to give TV and Radio a try. It sounds like a significant departure from drawing, but TV and Radio were avenues of expression that were out of reach to me before. I was really interested in those worlds, but couldn't get any closer than just being a spectator. College classes gave me a chance to give them a try. We live on a YouTube and podcast saturated planet now. It's straightforward for someone to make content and play the role of a star right from their own home. Back then, I could never have imagined the opportunities and outlets I would have as the technology developed. Words like "self-publish" or "independent label" had little or no meaning. Everything you did, from recording vocals for a song or editing a picture, required help from someone who spent thousands and thousands of dollars on equipment. Now we have all of that and more on a device that fits in our pocket. Technology makes me smile.

It was also around that time I got into DJing live vs. on-air. I wanted to explore both sides of the DJing world. One side involved a person actually mixing music in front of a live audience, the other where the person talked into a mic in between songs all alone in a broadcast studio. I figured you couldn't go wrong if you could do both. If you have both skills, you are twice as valuable and will have twice the opportunity. Like everything else in life, both types of DJing have their unique positives. One, the rush of the live crowd, the other has a disconnect from the live crowd but a distant connection to a much bigger audience further away.

It was also around that same time when I started competing in dance competitions, performing in dance shows, and teaching dance. It was just a year or so before I began making music and performing live as a vocalist. I was still doing physical art and still writing and working a day job. Around that time, there were 3 or 4 years I didn't own a TV. I just focused all my time on creating and performing. Like I said, life was a five-lane highway, and I had enough gas to drive on all five at top speed.

As a young person, I had a lot of freedom to create and loved it. Somewhere around then, I had to become an adult and move out on my own. The whole thought process of being creative started to be forced into a tiny box by the world around me. For some reason, everyone saw life only as what you did for a living. It didn't matter if you were happy just as long as you worked a respectable job and chased the picket fence dream. It was about how much you made, where you lived, and the family you raised. I was told more than once by "adults" around me,

"If you don't make something or fix something, it's not a real job."

I was told you weren't a grown-up unless you had your life on a specific plan that included working long hours, buying a home, and raising a family. Anything aside from that was just "playing," and you needed to "do something" with your life. Most of that talk came from people who were miserable because, at some point, they made a few poor decisions. Maybe they had a string of bad luck that put them in a position that didn't allow them to be who they wanted to be. Most likely, it was something simpler than that; it was a form of jealousy. I was being something they were afraid to be, my true self.

Please know, if you are in that place in life, I am not making fun of you. I do not want you to feel guilty for anything in the past. I want to encourage anyone who is, or was imprisoned by previous decisions, current difficulties, or self-doubt. You may feel like you crashed and burned a long time ago. You may feel your life is out of control now. You may feel there is no future and no hope. I want to tell you a truth about yourself that you may not be able to see or believe right now, but in the future, you will. You are doing better than you think, and you are not dead in the water. The Navy SEALs have a mindset about being done or finished. When you feel your tank is empty and you can't go any further, you still have 60 percent left. At that point, you are only about 40 percent maxed out. Your life is like what you are reading right now, just part of a book. This is not the end of the book, and neither is your life. Even if it's your last chapter, it's not the end of your book. Keep going till the final word is written.

This may be a bit extreme, but I had to do something around that time to get through life yet still be creative. Let me introduce you to someone that became a major part of my artistic life. His name is Michael Joseph. No, not me the person but Michael Joseph the persona. Life and people became very judgmental and mean, so to deal with all of that and feel more comfortable expressing my art, I created Michael Joseph. A persona to wear like a mask, so when the ugly side of the entertainment business hit home, it didn't feel so personal. It gave me a buffer zone between who I was and what I needed to do. I hope you don't have to create a totally different persona just to make it through each day. I hope some part of this book helps you to feel free and safe. Even if you only get to be creative for a couple of minutes drawing on a napkin at a restaurant, that's at least something that you can call your own.

Life has so many ups and downs. During many of those down times, my only expression and joy were those tiny pieces of paper. They might have been just tiny drawings or scribbles, but often they were the only cathartic moments I could get, and I took them. They felt good because everything was contained neatly inside the borders of the paper and everything around those drawings was a mess. I controlled the little that I could. I did the best I could with what I had in my hands at that time. Some days I might have felt I could move a mountain and tried with everything I had. It might have only been one shovel at a time, but that mountain was moving.

I want to define some avenues for income in my life as "day jobs." For most of my adult years, I almost always had a "day job" while I was chasing "the dream." I feel it is important to tell you that many of those day jobs had zero creativity. It seemed the jobs with zero creativity were the places I made the most money, had the best job benefits like vacation time, paid sick days, paid holidays, health care, and a retirement plan. Those were also the most challenging jobs for me to do and took an enormous toll on my mental and physical health. Without a doubt, they were the jobs I hated the most. It seemed there was some kind of sliding scale where I was exchanging my happiness for a solid income. They say money can't buy happiness, but in my life, it was giving up some of that money that gave me a different kind of wealth and happiness. I even had to define success and wealth differently. Creative freedom for me was just that ... freedom.

If you have ever felt the "day job" blues, you need to know you are not alone. Even though I really needed the income, I still felt like that "day job" was stealing my hope and destroying my humanity. It made me feel like I was on a far-off planet and didn't belong. Sometimes during lunch, I would just draw a picture while eating. It seemed to soften the sharp pain of the drudgery. For just a few minutes, I would lose myself in the picture and feel human again. Sometimes after work, I was creative just to wash the stench of the "day job" away. Being creative is what made me feel normal. I thought I was working to gain fame or money. I didn't know at that time, but it wasn't fame, money, or recognition I wanted. I just wanted to be creative, more specifically, make a living at being creative. It turned out the hunt for fame and fortune was just me constructing a self-narrative of the life I wanted through the art I made.

My outlet was in the traditional forms of creativity, but your avenue can be anything. When I talk about creativity, I'm not just talking about drawing, painting, writing, or typical artistic creativity. I'm talking about someone playing with a recipe to create a better flavor. Rebuilding an engine to make it more powerful is creativity. It's the carpenter who looks at a set of broken steps and, in their mind, creates a better set of steps. They may be the same size, shape, and color as the old steps, but they are now functional to the person and beautiful to the eye.

Creative expression can be anything. I've seen people write a brief note on a birthday or thank-you card that ended up being some of the most beautiful three or four words that I've ever read. Creativity can be a programmer or coder figuring out a clever way for an automated task. It could be a kind word that motivates a co-worker to believe their job is more than just a paycheck. Creativity can be used to complete just about every task. Thinking your way through a situation is one of the best creative journeys you can embark on. Also, you never know who you might encourage or help along that path.

An element of creativity is the hunger to better understand what you can't see. I have an insatiable "need" to understand how everything around me works. I think that is the lovechild between creativity and control. To some, that might be an ultimately futile waste of time and energy. To me, it's one of the things that makes life fun. I disassemble life to see if I'm doing something as well as it can be done. I'm looking at the smallest steps to streamline the process in the future. If you understand how something works, you have a better chance of fixing it when it breaks.

As we move forward to other chapters, I will talk about my creativity on paper, in the virtual realm, and in real life. I will describe temporary and permanent visual and audio moments as if they are living beings. I will show you creativity in the form of things like kind words, a helpful hand, or simply a smile. I hope by the end of this book, I not only help your creative process, but also your life. Maybe my creativity might help your creativity that then helps someone else's creativity. Who knows, their creativity might become a task or action that inspires me down the road, starting the entire circle over again.

Creativity should be a release, not just an action. In its purest form, it should pour out of you like sweat on a hot day. You can't stop it, and if you do, that wouldn't be healthy. Stifling creativity could cause you great harm. Keep in mind you don't have to make sense out of what you create. Just create and let it speak for itself. You will sometimes feel very vulnerable during the act of creating or sharing that creation with others. I warn you ahead of time that there will be people who won't understand. They will try to tear it down simply because they can't deal with it being different. The thing you create touches a spot inside them that hurts simply because, in life, they are not being the person they actually are on the inside. Don't let others impede your creativity just because they don't understand. Many people can't see the vision you can see. It isn't even a bad thing if they see something different from what you imagined. That is creativity in its rawest form. Your creativity helped them imagine something on its own.

As we continue on, I hope you will enjoy the journey and tour of my creative life. I hope you can take inspiration from the good things and the bad things that happen to me. I hope you will read through this as if we were sitting around talking about these things face to face. I hope I can explain these concepts about creativity and the journey I traveled. It may not be a well-defined roadmap like you were looking for. It may only be a simple compass bearing pointing you toward a single ray of hope on a dark day. Whatever happens, the journey is just that, a journey, but only if you step out and begin walking.

Chapter 3
Imagine Create Express

In the process of writing this book, I began looking at different ways I had been creative over the years. Was everything I did creativity or something totally different? I decided to look up the actual definition of the word creative. What I found was interesting. Definition one said, "having the quality or power of creating." That really wasn't much help, but definition two was: "Resulting from originality of thought, expression, etc.; imaginative." It put the word creative in the same thought as expression and imagination. I asked myself, are terms *creative*, *expressive*, and *imaginative* the same thing? Do you need one to have another or two of them to get the third? If you do, should one come before the other? Will this end up being like "the chicken or the egg" paradox? That, of course, caused me to do more research and overthink something that shouldn't be thought about, just experienced.

In my opinion, creativity, expression, and imagination can all be used simultaneously, just like they can all exist totally separate from each other. There is no single recipe for mixing the three to create a masterpiece. I'm not even sure there is a tangible formula that fits every person or situation. To even begin trying to figure this out, I first had to understand what times in my life I was creative vs. imaginative vs. expressive.

This entire project came about when I realized I was chasing the need to be creative. Looking back, I saw that imagining and expressing were just as important. Often the three changed top billing when it came to how others looked at my final projects. All three were always around but not labeled for a specific use or recipe. I took each one as needed and instinctively let it do its own function for that job. Since I think in pictures, I broke down different actions and looked at them from an outside perspective. I tried to label the action or see if it had a formula using any combination of creativity, expression, or imagination.

Let's look at a baby having a temper tantrum. That is an extremely expressive act, but how much creativity or imagination was put into that moment of expression? Maybe not a lot, but it is within the boundaries of what a child's intellect can draw from as a means to get them what they want. Is the level of creativity connected to the level of expression? Do you need one to have the other? Was the expressive act first imagined? Could any of this be labeled creative?

I'm guessing there aren't any babies reading this book, so what about the rest of us? We also have similar deep-rooted forms of expression called knee-jerk reactions. I have a lot of experience with this form of expression. I express how I feel in that moment through what seems to be a conscious or pre-planned reaction. It might be how I truly feel, even though I wish I could filter it in a better way. I expressed myself, but did I create it from thought or as a defense mechanism of a previous experience? If I don't like how I reacted, can I imagine or create a better way of expression the next time it happens? If you need to take an aspirin at this point, I totally understand.

Did you take your aspirin? Ok then, let's go further. When I looked at the fine line between expressive and creative,

I saw the only thing that separates them may be the motivation of the act. Let's say you are just expressing yourself as a means of therapy. You are not trying to convey a thought or specific instruction; you are not trying to make something for others to enjoy; you are not trying to evoke an emotion; you are not doing any of this with the thought of giving or showing it to anyone. In the end, you might very well create something beautiful through the act of catharsis, but to you, that would be more expressive than creative.

Imagination can be highly therapeutic without expression or creativity. It lets you detach from your current surroundings as a means of escape or retreat. Daydreaming is more common than you think. Studies show that the average person spends 47% of their awake time daydreaming, even while multitasking. Some might say it's a silly waste of time, but some of the best inventions and ideas came from moments of unrestricted and unscheduled daydreaming. Sometimes you just have to "Go to your happy place."

Being in the middle of a creative moment can be both comforting and alarming. You quickly forget about the world around you. It's happening at a speed that is faster than real-time. Coming from the center of your core, it moves outward. It takes up pretty much all points in space and time from the center out. You can easily get lost in it yet quickly find your way back. To your brain, the reality of imagining is just as tangible as the physical world. Don't believe me? Try imagining a barking dog, a giant spider, or standing on a tall cliff. You felt something, didn't you? None of it was real, but when you imagined it, your mind reacted, and your body felt like it was. That power of imagination can not only be used to create something beautiful but also be used to overcome fears or just escape a boring conversation.

Not many people truly understand what it's like to be deep in a creative moment. Some might call it getting in the zone. The best I can describe is when the whole world around you melts away except for the singular act you are attempting to complete. Many athletes describe the zone as a regular part of their game. I once heard a boxer say he knew the exact moment when it was time for him to retire. He said, "I saw where I wanted to punch and then threw the punch." The interviewer pointed out that very same punch won him the fight. The boxer said, "True, but when I was younger, my subconscious would have been in the zone, saw where to punch, and then threw the punch before my conscious mind saw it." His punch was a chosen response instead of a natural reaction in the zone.

That's probably why I love playing sports so much. When in the zone, you forget about absolutely everything aside from that moment. You don't think about troubles or stress over life. You don't rehash old conversations or things you wish you did differently. At that moment, all of those things lose their grip on your mind. For those few moments, you are truly free. The act, in itself, is beyond a therapeutic description. It's one of those times I heard someone describe as "If I have to explain, you wouldn't understand."

If your brain isn't hurting by now, how about this? Is the zone an all-or-nothing way of thinking or a complete release of both all and nothing at the same time? Even if you don't play sports, you have experienced it before. It's when you get totally lost in what you're doing. You focus so intensely, someone could be talking to you or even throwing things at you, and you don't even know they were there. You were focusing on one thing and nothing at the same time. It's not a fixed point of focus. Most of the time, your mind is alert to many things going on in the room, yet also choosing to focus on one thing. That is one of the hardest things for me to do. Focus on one thing and block the unneeded or unwanted out. That skill is just as important to problem-solving as it is to creating art.

It may not seem like it, but problem-solving is one of my favorite forms of creativity. It starts with the intellect identifying a problem. Then, your imagination begins to piece together pictures that show different paths and outcomes. If free of distraction, your creativity works to find an outcome with the desired result. Once that process comes to a near-complete idea, you can then express the solution your mind came up with. From beginning to end, it might take tenths of a second or decades to reveal itself. I've even seen that whole thing work in reverse. The solution presented itself first, but you have to wait for new technology to catch up before putting the entire thing together.

Concepts of creative problem solving have been debated to death. Convergent Thinking and Divergent Thinking were terms coined by Joy Paul Guilford. Convergent thinking says that there is one "best" way to solve a problem. Divergent thinking says you should explore many possible solutions to the same problem. I think a really creative mind sees both at the same time … plus a few other factors. It's very multidimensional to a genuinely free creative mind. All the paths are overlaid on a three-dimensional space in a perceived reality. A great example of imagination and creativity working, in reality, comes from the movie *Iron Man*. Tony Stark takes apart and rebuilds the Iron Man suit on what seems to be a tangible and physical model right in front of him. It's a 3D render, of course, but that is how a creative mind works. Remember the dog barking, giant spider, and tall cliff experiment? It may not be real to you, but it's real to the person feeling it.

You have now entered "the imagination dimension." Not only is your mind seeing all the variables coming in at a high rate of speed, but it is calculating in past experiences and the probability of where each one of those factors will finish. It sees both the incoming and the outgoing on multiple levels at the same time. You can both see one way of doing something that gets several different results and several ways of doing something that gets one result. I call that "multivergent thinking," you heard it here first.

The brain does its own sorting and filtering on a subconscious level. For example, imagine you are in a busy coffee shop. The general noise of the entire room will tend to blend together and wash over you unconsciously. That scenario drives some people crazy, but for many others, it helps them focus. Believe it or not, it becomes a "distraction" to help you "focus." That is often called a form of Flexible or Leaky Attention. That is not only done with outside stimuli but also with your inner dialog. The mind can have its own internal gating of thoughts that are unnecessary or redundant. In the problem-solving process, that mindset can eliminate objects or actions that are either unavailable or unusable in the real-life solution at this time.

Some people work better like that. Mixing the gating of internal dialog and outward stimuli. They feel more relaxed when there is white noise playing in the background. Leaky thinking is where your mind only lets certain pieces of information from the real world in and others stay out. The mind balances the external input as it prioritizes some of the inner dialogs for a solution. It kinda works on its own extra-dimensional plane. Back to the Tony Stark example, it gives motion and reaction to ideas as if they were physical objects right in front of you.

The creative mind can walk into a situation and begin working towards the solution before we realize it. Before someone asks our thoughts, our mind somehow has figured out several desirable outcomes. Some people think of it as an instant light bulb moment. The truth is there are a countless number of steps going on before that "light bulb" flashing. It's happening on a subconscious level without interrupting outward actions. It's as if we see the big picture from an out-of-body experience. The mind is not restricted by rules, only guided by previous experiences. A self-guided subconscious calculation through endless probabilities to a logical solution.

In short, you're able to take everything in at a millisecond, then filter it and express it in real-time. Your mind sees where each piece of the puzzle fits, but you still have to pick each one up and put it in the right place. The creative mind sees the solution to the problem worked out before the process actually starts. Maybe that is why some creatives get bored quickly. We don't need to complete the physical puzzle because we have already finished it in our mind. We don't need to waste all that time physically piecing it together. We just move on to the next creative challenge.

This way of thinking and seeing life may be a foreign concept to most people, but to a person who relies on creativity, this happens every moment of every day. We find ourselves being creative, or at least treating each process we do creatively. We imagine, during mundane things, like tying our shoes, and even imagine every step we will take that day. In the creative mind, they all have ever-changing possibilities. Some think using your brainpower in this way is a waste of time, effort, or energy, but to stop the creative mind from doing this will bring that person's life to a crashing halt.

A creative person can work and even sometimes flourish in that way of thinking. It removes some rules and guidelines and replaces them with a gating system you can't see. One thing that I have heard so many people talk about is that fear kills creativity. Some people even describe fear as a creativity inhibitor. However, you choose to describe it, fear causes us to second-guess even our gut feelings. Fear is a negative gate. This gate may be forced on us by others in our lives, or we illogically put it there ourselves. Either way, unless you deal with that gate, it will forever make you feel hopeless, without options, and fenced in.

The best you can do is give the creative mind some guidelines and rules. With those guidelines, it can then figure out what variables can and can't be altered in the equation. It can't imagine, create, and express if it fears a hostile reaction. The feedback needs to be at least constructive in some manner. Good guidelines usually come when one person is making the final decision. That person can clearly express to the creative person what is expected of them. We will call that person "the good guide." The good guide also has to hold themselves accountable for the decisions or changes they make along the process. In short, just tell us if you want us to lead, follow or get out of the way.

One of the hardest things for me to watch is someone with a creative mind dealing with someone that assumes everyone thinks as they do. To me, that way of thinking is a type of prejudice. You prejudge others by presuming they think like you. If you presume then get mad at someone or make fun of them for thinking differently, you are now bullying them. The bully judges because the other person doesn't think like them. The bully then corrects authoritatively until it's done the bully's way. That person is a manipulator, and I will go into detail about them in a future chapter.

I don't think it matters how you individually or collectively use creativity, expression, and imagination. Each is a tremendous tool to have in your toolbox. Each has its own amazing potential. Each can be a treasured ally if given room to breathe. Give each of them guidelines and rules when needed and let them run free when you can. You will never regret the extra effort it takes to be a good guide. Even if the rest of the world is trying to imprison you with fear or nurture your creative self with love and compassion. It doesn't matter if you want to make art, solve problems, or just navigate your way through life;

embrace your inner creative, expressive, and imaginative self.

Chapter 4
More Than Art

When I say the word "creativity," people will almost always think of art or entertainment. That form is the most popular final product of creativity, but actually, its baseline is so much more. To me, creativity is not the final product but the core to just about everything in life. Every problem you have, every emotion you experience, and every path you take is strewn with creativity in one manner or another. It's a part of our hopes, our dreams, our blessings, and our schemes. Used for good or bad, creativity begins before the first thought and keeps going after the job is done. In this chapter, I want to examine how creativity is the foundation of so many things in life that have nothing to do with "art."

Many things that are a part of our daily lives came about by accident. Penicillin, the Slinky, the pacemaker, and even chocolate chip cookies were all positive results of a failed attempt. The difference is someone decided to take the actual results they got and find new uses for them. 3M scientist Dr. Spencer Silver was attempting to develop a new strong adhesive. In that process, he came up with a low-tack adhesive that was reusable. During one of Dr. Silver's seminars, one of the attendees by the name of Art Fry came up with the idea to use the new adhesive to hold the bookmark in his hymnal from constantly falling out. Two moments of separate creativity gave us post-it notes. Now people all over the world use them every day in their own creative journey.

During World War II, scientists were trying to develop a new synthetic rubber replacement. During that process, they came up with a formula that not only stretched more than rubber, bounced more than rubber but also broke like a solid when struck hard. Not to mention this strange substance acted like liquid when left alone. Many of us know this as a toy called Silly Putty, but through creativity, it has been used to remove dirt, ink, or other substances from surfaces or hard-to-reach places. It is often used by occupational therapists for rehabilitation therapy that involves the hands. Apollo astronauts used it to secure tools in zero gravity, and some people even mold it in their hands as a means to reduce stress.

You might say those things were more discovered than created, and that would be partially right. What do you call finding a use for something way different from what you had intended? I call it creativity. It's nothing more than thinking outside the box. As a person matures, their brain develops an understanding that a particular object has a given function. This is called "functional fixedness." In layman's terms, it's the right tool for the right job. Creativity is the freedom from that thought pattern. Creativity means your mind can generate new and unique ways or paths around an obstacle to a solution or explanation. Typical forms of art like music, painting, or sculpting use creativity in a very un-seen blueprint. Creativity used in problem-solving often shows that blueprint in a well-defined step-by-step solution.

Some often say the only difference between art and problem-solving is how much room each has for interpretation. One person can call it good art, while another says it's not art at all. Can you view a task artistically? Is there an artistic difference between a job well done versus phoning it in? They both may have the same conclusion, and both are filled with testing, learning, and creative problem-solving. The only difference is how each is perceived. The mind of the viewer and creator may see both art and a completed task at the same time or only one of them. Personal interpretation is the only separating factor. I know that is a super simplistic view but try looking at a specific object viewed in different situations.

I grew up on a small farm. On our tractor, we had a toolbox that permanently kept basic tools if you were out in the field and needed to fix something. My father always kept a very large crescent wrench in that toolbox. It was an adjustable wrench that was often used precisely how that type of wrench was intended. Just as many times, it was used for everything but what it was intended. It was a hammer pounding in fence staples (we pronounced it "steeples"). Many times, it was a pry bar. It was used as an extension to some other sort of device to increase leverage. I've even seen it used as a measuring device because my father knew its exact length.

In the medical world, using something other than what it's intended for is known as off-label usage, taking a drug labeled explicitly for a particular treatment and using its benefits to help a totally different problem. Reasons for off-label usage could be anything from the right medicine isn't currently available, or the patient's health insurance doesn't cover the proper prescription. Either way, the off-label drug will often get the same desired outcome.

Next time you're at the drugstore, take a moment and look at the label on the drug Benadryl right next to an over-the-counter sleeping pill label. Both are the same dosage of diphenhydramine. There are many other over-the-counter off-label examples. We all know what Preparation H is intended for, but it's often administered by dermatologists to reduce puffiness under the eyes. Many people still take aspirin daily to lower the risk of a heart attack. The off-label use of medication isn't talked about too openly, yet it is very common.

One of the most off-label used tools in the world is Duct Tape. It was originally created during World War 2 to seal around ammunition cases to keep them dry. Most people just use it as a way of holding two things together, but its real-life possibilities are nearly endless. I've seen people use it as a makeshift rope to repel down a cliff. I've seen it used to make a hammock. There is even a competition worth $20,000 for the students who make the best prom attire out of Duck Tape brand duct tape. It's a well-known fact amongst farmers that you only need four things in your toolbox, duct tape, baling twine, WD-40, and a hammer … or in my dad's case, also a large crescent wrench.

The effectiveness of the "off-label" style of creativity is only limited by your mental freedom. I once saw someone temporarily plug a hole at the end of a water pipe with a spark plug because the threads matched. It's also well known that you can stop a small leak in your car's radiator by pouring household pepper in with the antifreeze. How many people have used a butter knife as a screwdriver or a garbage bag as a rain poncho? How many times have you propped open a door with something that was not intended to hold a door open?

This way of thinking comes naturally to my brain. I tend to see dual purposes in everything, especially when it comes to having fun. My grandfather taught me how to make a whistle by putting a single blade of grass between my thumbs placed side by side. Many of us (to our teacher's dismay) made folded paper "firecrackers" when we were younger. Take the cardboard container, your fries come in at McDonald's. The bottom is folded upwards to give the container some rigidity. If you push the bottom down, place a small piece of fry there, then squeeze the sides in just the right way, the bottom of the container will pop up, and the fry will fly in the air. Catch the fry back in the container and repeat. If you have a friend who also has a container, you can play catch back and forth. A straw can be an excellent delivery method to many types of beverages, but what do you do when you are finished using that straw? You should recycle it of course, but before you do, roll up the ends to create a compressed pocket of air in the center. Then have someone flick the center of that pocket; it will make a loud popping sound. Don't believe me; just look up a YouTube video on how it's done.

While we are on the subject of food, let's look at creativity in cooking. Many people have made prominent names for themselves with this type of creativity. From some of the most accomplished chefs in the world to how creatively Sheldon's mother (from The Big Bang Theory) would put hot dogs in his spaghetti. If you haven't given that a try, I highly recommend you do. Not that I have ever cooked one but tell me the turducken isn't creatively awesome. Have you ever seen the Meals in a Mug way of cooking? As a single person who hates to cook, I can tell you it's actually a fun way to make a quick single-serving meal, side dish, or dessert.

Food can serve a purpose beyond eating. If done right, you can turn half an orange peel and some olive oil into a makeshift candle. Cut the orange in half sideways, remove the fruit out of the peel but leave the stem attached. Now fill the orange peel about halfway with olive oil and light the stem. First a food source, now a light source. Many people have used dried gourds as a storage container, ladles, or even a musical instrument. Let us not forget the many uses of the Myristica tree. Nutmeg is made from its seed, and mace is made from the seed's covering. I think most people prefer the seed over the covering.

Thinking outside the box really comes down to looking at all the possible options instead of just trying to find a solution. Don't start with a fixed ending point. Instead, begin with what you have and where that could go. That could be an overwhelming number of directions but be willing to at least look at all of them before you decide on one. Eliminating even one possibility without trying to see where it leads could be eliminating the one that works best.

Sometimes you find yourself with too much of one thing and not enough of another. That is when creativity can turn a loss or overstock into a win. Think of it like assembling a jigsaw puzzle. You could put all the pieces together to see the picture or just complete the puzzle for the fun of it. Artist Tim Klein discovered that many puzzle-manufacturing companies often use the same die to cut different puzzles. Since these pieces matched in shape, Klein started mixing different puzzles and creating whole new scenes. Is this a failure because the puzzle doesn't look like the picture on the box or a win because both puzzles were completed?

Sometimes being creative with art is not art. Sometimes the act of creating becomes therapy. Studies show that doing something creative for just 45 minutes a day can lower stress levels. I've known many people that took the task of rebuilding a car or tackling a large project as therapy for getting past a major life problem. The finished project is just a bonus to the healing power gained by focusing on the task. The task becomes self-healing through being creative. The space between the beginning and the end of a project is where you often find an answer to a question you always wanted to know or the life path you were always meant to travel.

The room you give your mind to create can often be determined by the thoughts you allow yourself to dwell on. The numbers vary depending on who you ask, but on average, a person has between 12,000 and 60,000 thoughts per day. Believe it or not, about 80% of those thoughts each day are about something negative. You may say that is a little alarming, but the crazy number is that the studies also showed 95% of those thoughts were exactly the same thoughts as the day before. Breaking a habit is hard work, but if you do, you could change your entire outlook, which will then make room for unrestricted creativity.

One way to heal your mind from those destructive, repetitive thoughts is to give it something else to focus on. You must pick a task that is bigger than that moment and requires multiple steps for completion. The act of creating can be a part of that process. One way I have found to change my temporary focus is through sports. You might not think of sports as creative, but you would be surprised. Many of the tasks in sports require you to creatively outthink the opponent. Fake right and then go left, the no-look pass, the flea-flicker. Many elaborate successful plays in sports result in a team creating a way to work together and outplay their opponent. One of the best side effects of playing sports is that you often have to be so "in the moment" during play that you can't think about anything else. The physical act creates the need for mental focus that over time gives your brain a break to reboot. Not to mention better physical health has shown to lead to better mental health.

It doesn't always take a big plan to be creative. Just try making something from only the things at your disposal. Those things might be the free time of a single person or someone in a pandemic lockdown. It could be the physical space you own or have access to. It could be people in your life that can join in the process. It could be resources or knowledge at your fingertips. Most likely, it comes down to the sheer need to change something. Many things can push you towards the needed change. It could be your surroundings or what is going on inside. It could be an unhealthy situation you are stuck in. Sometimes the best motivation for positive change in our life comes from the sheer need to escape a horrible situation. It could be a bad relationship or just a job that stresses you so much you are becoming physically sick. Using the need for changes as your creative inspiration can be worth more than the best-laid plans.

One of my favorite parts of writing this book was the nights that I just sat at the desk and spoke from the heart. I was not trying to convey a single point, but I was more or less describing a situation from my point of view. Think of it as someone walking around a table trying to describe a bouquet of flowers in the center. As you shuffle to the right or to the left around the table, a different view gives you a fresh perspective. That is precisely how a lot of this journey has been for me. It wasn't a giant spark of lightning, but a simple shift of perspective. It might take some work to see things in a new light. But the hard work is going to be worth it even if you don't achieve your exact goals. The journey itself often builds character that becomes the catalyst to a second wind. You would be amazed in life what new opportunities show up right after a new outlook does.

Things could look great to others, but you may be dying on the inside. You could achieve all your goals in life and still feel empty. I once heard someone say that they accomplished everything in life they wanted, but then realized they didn't really want any of it. No one can make someone else happy. You can make someone laugh or smile, but often unhappiness can only be gotten rid of by making a choice to stop holding it. Once we let go of one thing, then and only then can we pick up other things we want. It could be a better relationship with someone or just a little peace of mind in a situation. You and only you can get you to where you want to be. Don't be surprised if it takes a lot of creativity to achieve your first step. It may take an elaborate plan that involves taking chances and adapting to the results. No matter the plan or path, you can use creativity to find a solution to work through and achieve your goals. It may come down to you just getting out of your own way.

Chapter 5
Eye See Different

It took several decades of being alive until I realized I saw life differently than most people. Ideas and thoughts become a series of pictures. Not static pictures on the wall but more like a series of images in motion used to describe a word, an idea, or even a whole story. To a visual thinker, everything in life is related to some sort of visual image in our minds. When we work through a problem, these pictures take up space and have motion. They create a living storyboard showing all possible outcomes and paths.

I once heard Temple Grandin described this process as a "Google picture search." Something said or seen triggers the "search." Suddenly, everything you have previously viewed or imagined about that topic comes into your mind. It's like a page populating from all sides, with pictures like in a search engine, but they are alive, and each tells its own story. To answer or understand what they are saying, you first have to put some of them together. A combination of different parts assembled to become a more defined idea of the original trigger. This assembly of pictures can also be used to construct new ideas. It is creativity in its original point of creation.

Sometimes this way of thinking is extremely beneficial, but other times it can be a major hindrance. Beneficial in the sense that you can see stuff laid out and understand long before everyone else does. You can see how a situation is going to play itself out steps ahead. It's beneficial in terms of understanding how something works even without removing a single part. It was said that

Nikola Tesla worked on some of his inventions this way, tearing each down and reassembling them over and over in his mind until he was able to fix the problem in the real world.

It can become a hindrance when those thoughts get between you and a person or thing you need to focus on. It can interrupt a conversation or derail a task that needs to be completed. It changes the original priority of tasks, leaving a previous center point of focus completely out of the picture. To the outside world, this may seem rude or selfish. It becomes an attention-hungry third person in a previous two-way conversation. It makes time stop on the inside while blind to the interrupting chaos it causes in the real world. In short, some days, it's an all-out war for my attention.

It even affects the metaphysical world by helping you see through someone else's eyes. You can feel and empathize a little more deeply with a self-created new perspective. I remember one time during one of the photography classes I took in high school; the teacher asked everyone to put their photo project for that week on the chalkboard ledge. We each took turns picking out our favorite picture in the room. I picked out one that was very blurry. The person did not intend to take a blurry photograph. It was just a mistake, but I saw the motion of light as the composition in my mind. That photograph, in its imperfect form, created a very well-balanced and expressive collection of light and color. It just made for a beautiful artistic picture. I understood something that the photographer didn't even know they were saying.

If planned out, you can speak words to someone through a picture on a subconscious level. One of the best lessons I learned in photography class is the positioning of subjects in an image. The subject isn't always a person; sometimes it's a building, others just the direction of the shadow or light. You start to look at everything in the scene to see if it can be changed by moving the camera's perspective. As westerners, we read left to right, so to have a scene read or appear natural, you will set the picture to read left to right. The opposite composition can be used to convey the idea of "wrong" or "rethink." Often the test of good composition is when the image can read well when viewed as a regular or reversed image.

A common practice in TV and Movies is to stage a conversation either left to right or right to left. The person who is to be prominent in the exchange is always on the left side facing right. It makes the scene read left to right and brings the person on the left to the virtual forefront of the conversation. That's why most talk shows have their guests sitting on the left side of the screen facing right. This is done for more than just aesthetics. It tricks the mind into automatically giving prominence and importance to the guest.

Pay attention the next time you are watching a movie or TV show to where characters are standing while talking. You will often see them switch places in mid-conversation. That is done when one-character changes from being the dominant speaker in the conversation, facing right, to the weaker or secondary character facing left. This is often expressed by having the hero face right and the villain face left. It is a subconscious narrative that causes a reaction in the brain you don't even realize. You are being manipulated into giving one person power over the other.

This way of composition can also be used in the real world. During my years of live performances, I had DJ equipment that needed to be set up on the stage. Because I shared the stage with other bands, I had to put my DJ gear out of the way of their instruments yet still be able to access it quickly. I started putting my gear on the left side of the stage from the audience's point of view. That gave me the prominent position when it came to the eye line on the stage. It gave me an "attention first" view on a subconscious level.

When laying out a flyer or poster, most people would say top billing is what you want, but it isn't always best if the area around the top billing is cluttered. Sometimes being below in an empty space at the bottom corner lets you stand out more. Even being the last name on a list that someone sees will often stick in their mind more than the first. Everything in life has patterns, and once you learn the different thoughts and emotions that those patterns evoke, you can then start layering them to create an entire story just from a few colors on a page. Try setting up the ending of your story subconsciously before they even read the first word. With some simple editing, you can completely change the emotional effect to the opposite side of the spectrum from where it started.

As technology became a big part of my creativity, I discovered photo editing software. It's really nice to take a photograph and manipulate it to look exactly the way you intended it to. If you don't like where a cloud is, you move the cloud. You can flip the picture to create an aesthetic left to right read. You can change the contrast or saturation to make it feel warmer or deeper. To get that picture to look right without the post-editing tools used to take a lot of work, a good eye, and some creativity. Don't get me wrong, creativity is still very much needed in the editing process, but the more setup you do before the picture is taken will reduce the amount you need to edit in the end.

Let's talk about the type of picture a lot of people take daily, the selfie. Unless you are an Instagram ninja, you probably don't take a lot of time to set up your selfie. You just take a bunch of pictures and choose the one you like best. If you pay attention to your surroundings and put in a little extra effort, you can create an image you want without using the editing software; not always, but sometimes you do have to be lucky to catch that right moment for that right emotion with the lens. What I'm talking about is where you stop being the subject or the photographer. You start being the editor before the picture is even taken. Many of the Instagram stars plan out selfies days or weeks in advance. They pay for lighting, sets, and props to make that picture memorable yet seemingly effortless.

Not being the subject of the photograph can help you start seeing ways to improve your selfies. If you change how comfortable someone is while taking the photograph, it can totally change how it reads. Edit (or manipulate) the emotion before you take the picture. Think about creating something that they want to share. Think about creating something that a total stranger would like to stop and look at. It may take a little emotional hacking to get someone to smile or relax, but it can be the difference between just taking a photograph of a person to having a subject alive and breathing in your picture. That also includes making yourself feel the emotion you want to convey. Find something that makes you laugh or smile before taking a happy picture. Think of a hard time in your life when you need to capture the seriousness of depth. Hack your own emotions when you need to but remember to chill out in the end; it's just a selfie.

Another powerful tool is how color evokes emotion. Go online sometime and look up how different brands choose their logo colors to reach a specific audience. Colors alone can embody distinct traits. The colors can be feminine or masculine, youthful or mature, aggressive or subdued, playful, or serious. Many food brands choose the color red for their logo to give off the emotion of passion, love, hunger, health, and life. Other brands choose blue to convey professionalism, loyalty, or trust. Your eye sees, your brain reacts, and you didn't even notice. You were just manipulated into an emotion or decision just by something's color.

If you are the subject in the art you are creating, you as a person, just like the brands, can choose clothing colors to evoke an emotion or feeling before the picture is taken. Do you want someone to notice you, or do you want them to notice what you're wearing? Do you want to be seen, or do you want to blend in? You can also set up a predetermined point of focus to distract the eye away to add subtlety. It's even fun sometimes to hide little things within the photograph as a special Easter egg to reward those who really pay attention. This is where the

Instagram pro tells a complete and complex story with a quick snapshot.

All of these things make up a simple baseline of creativity. Instead of just looking at the subject in the center of the frame, look everywhere around it to create a bigger picture or make sure that your subject is the only thing to focus on. Imagine what you currently see framed differently. Add or eliminate something in the background to change the depth or scale. Imagine a cropped head-to-toe photo or drawing of someone standing in a field. Now imagine the same image zoomed way back to include a giant tornado in the background. The subject can be smiling in both pictures yet have totally different emotional reactions from the viewer. The close-up image shows a happy person, while the wide-angle shows a person who may look crazy or foolish for smiling when they are obviously in danger.

Take all of these things and put them into life as you walk around each day. Change where you stand when you meet someone to have a real-life effect. Change the direction you're walking towards them to create backlighting or front lighting to enhance your first impression. When you sit down at a table, try to sit where there's no movement behind the people you are sitting with so you can focus. Or put nothing behind you, so they don't get distracted. It doesn't matter if it's a drawing, a photo, a movie, or real life; the mind is still affected by what it sees. You, as the creator, can "create" and make the moment seem like so much more. It may be a lie or manipulation, but perspective is always subjective to the viewer. If we see different sides to the same coin, remember, there is still just one coin, yet two ideas.

Chapter 6
Dance Or Die

Even before I knew I loved dancing, I loved dancing. If you can't stand still when you hear music, then you totally understand that statement. If you have ever tripped while walking because in your mind you were doing choreography, you get it. If everything starts with "5, 6, 7, 8", then you love dancing too. It has definitely been an all-consuming fire in my creative world at times. For some people, dancing falls in between creative and expressive. For me, it is by far the purest form of expression. Of all my creative outlets, it makes me the happiest and, by far, is the most therapeutic. Until I stopped and took a deeper look at dancing, I didn't know how much it has helped me in the past and is still helping to this day.

You might not think of dancing as an act that helps you on multiple levels inside and out. It's just something fun to do. Expressing yourself via dance is so much more than just having fun. If you have spent any time dancing, I don't have to tell you about its benefits. Dancing helps the psychological, the physical, and the chemical parts of the dancer. It nourishes both the body and the mind. Dancing can be used to connect with other people, and that connection can improve your state of being and self-esteem. Dancing can help on a chemical level as it releases dopamine and serotonin. They are chemicals that reduce stress and increase the feeling of happiness. It has been proven that dancing makes your brain age slower by reducing the shrinkage of the hippocampus that naturally comes with aging.

Dancers have a better sense of their spatial parameters and how to navigate them more instinctively. From the repeated movement of the body, a dancer's muscles gain a faster awareness of position and direction. If the dancer were blindfolded, they would have a better sense of where someone moved them in the room or how far they walked without visual feedback. If you had that blindfolded dancer stand on a flat surface then change the angle of that flat surface, the dancer would have a better ability to stay upright as the angle underneath their feet changed. As the human body ages, many people have difficulty balancing or walking in a straight line. Dancers have a better sense of an imagined external focal point, thus maintaining better balance and steady tracking as they walk.

For me, dancing has helped on all of these levels at different stages of my creative journey. It has always been a recharging act for my internal batteries. It has healed me on the inside over and over throughout my career. I can't imagine what my life would be like without dancing. It's not always been easy on a cultural level. Dancing isn't something a lot of "men" where I grew up with did. I've never been one to let the opinion of others stop me from chasing my goals and dreams. If you will, please journey with me back in time to explore the significant moments in my life that involved dancing. I want to single them out in this chapter because I feel they were my foundation for all my other acts of creativity. It may not seem like much, but each of these "times of dance" in my past kept me sane, happy, and moving forward. I owe a lot to dance, and that is why I want to share these moments with you. I hope by the end you will be able to see the importance of moving with the music should be to your life as well.

There were five points along the path of my dance life that were gravitational slingshots pushing me deeper into the expressive universe. If you excuse the pun, my first steps into dance began during the era of breakdancing. It was an extremely unique form of dance. There had been nothing like it up till that point. It wasn't a variation or twist of some other form. It was so unique that it became the catalyst for many of my future artistic expressions.

One of the things that drew me to breakdancing is that it didn't require a partner or other people you danced in unison with. It was something that was performance-based, yet didn't require a band, a building, or even chairs for an audience to sit and watch. We danced pretty much anywhere we had a smooth floor or could put down some cardboard. Unlike ballet that requires the classic moves to be executed precisely the same each time, breakdancing also had universal dance moves, but you were praised when you changed them slightly to show your own unique style.

I was pretty young when breakdancing became popular. At that time, my main creative/expressive outlet was mainly drawing. Dancing was such a departure from my norm. I'm not even sure why I gravitated towards it so much. It was like I had a need to pursue it. I found myself trying to learn breakdance moves from other dancers who were much better than me. I would get together with friends who lived somewhat near me to practice. So many people forget about the social aspect of dancing. Total strangers can connect over dancing of any type. If you want to see one of the most complex and diverse social scenes built around dancing, go to a local Salsa night. The diversity of age, gender, race, religion, geography, economics, and skill levels makes it one of the most all-inclusive melting pots of the dance world.

The second slingshot step of expression happened the summer after I graduated from high school. A friend of mine invited me to go to an under-21 dance. He talked about how hot the room got and how much it cost to get in, as if those were selling points. I thought to myself, there's no way I'm going to pay money to go sweat in public. After he and several other friends continued to tell me what I was missing out on each and every week, I finally gave in. I told them, "If I go once, never ask me to go again." Little did I know that paying money to sweat in public as I danced was going to be an undeniable, lifelong passion.

From the first night I showed up, I was hooked. Trying to learn the different dance moves and realizing I was quite good at them; it became somewhat addictive. If I wasn't dancing, I was thinking about dancing. Going somewhere each week to move with the music became a necessity. I even remember skipping lunches to ensure that I had enough gas and entrance money for that weekend. It didn't even matter if the weather was terrible; I had to get there. I did whatever it took and made room in my life to go dancing each weekend.

My ability and skills grew faster than I could have imagined. I was having so much fun. It wasn't long before I found myself entering dance competitions at different clubs around the area. The competitions became the third slingshot point I spoke of earlier. It just made me want to dance more. There were so many incredibly talented people that loved dancing as much as I did. Everywhere I went, I found seas of people to connect with over dancing.

Believe it or not, I won every dance competition I entered aside from two. In both of those, I took second place. One of those second-place battles was against two guys named Sean and Chris. Later on, the three of us became great friends and even danced in TV commercials together. After the competition that night, I asked them about their routine and how they put it together. They told me they danced for a company called the Joyce Ellis dancers and invited me to come to one of the practices. This was the fourth slingshot point in my life where things changed dramatically. I went from hanging out with friends who loved dancing to having a dance family.

I showed up to the first class and was immediately hooked. There was only one problem, this wasn't me going to dance club battles in the city 45 minutes away. I lived in a small town where people tended to judge you a lot. It takes us back to the saying I told you earlier "Unless you make something or fix something, you don't really work, you only take from others who do work." That thought pattern set very heavily on my mind as I debated whether to join the dance company and try to "chase a dream." This was such a departure from many I grew up with. If I did this, I knew I would be singling myself out amongst many around me.

For me, to step out of the drawing mentality and move on to the dance floor was one thing, but to then join a company and get on a stage to put on shows seemed almost crazy. A mature person didn't "chase silly dreams" like that. You were supposed to go to college, get a real job, and a "real" life. I remember sitting down and talking to some of my friends about wanting to pursue dancing. I got a couple of positive, encouraging statements, but most of them just bit their tongues. I don't think they wanted to say how they truly felt. In their minds, "real men" didn't do "artsy" things like that. I spent a lot of time trying to make my mind up if I should start taking dance classes or not. In hindsight, my choice was as clear as could be. I already knew it wasn't a matter of should, but that I had to. I remember a popular T-shirt at that time that read "Dance or Die." On the inside, it truly felt like it was one or the other, and it simply wasn't time to die.

Officially starting with the Joyce Ellis Dancers was quite intimidating. There were a lot of very talented dancers. Some of them had even performed on TV and in stadiums. To my advantage, the dance style in the clubs at that time was trendy, so I knew what I was doing in the clubs would be popular on stage. That style allowed me to do a lot of special shows. One of the first showcases I did for Joyce was with Sean, Chris, and myself. We did a couple of routines at a local NAACP youth meeting. I was extremely nervous but still felt very accepted. I still have the video from that night, and when the music starts, you can see where I almost missed the first move of the dance because of the nerves. That night turned out to be one of the coolest nights in my dance career.

Joyce was very connected throughout the entertainment world, so we got a lot of amazing opportunities. We danced on TV shows and even for a series of commercials. I danced with the company for several years. I felt a lot of pressure from people around me to live a more "normal life." They would say things like "you're too old to be chasing those childish dreams" or "when are you going to settle down." For a while, I tried my best to hide amongst the naysayers. I tried to fit in and still be creative, but stopping the creativity altogether was not going to happen.

You will see a pattern in my life where I finish one type of creativity and quickly move on to something else. I wanted to expand on the dancing skills I learned and see how far I could go. I wanted to take that dance expression into another dimension, vocal performance. That's when I started writing lyrics and music. In my mind, the background in dance would add up to a powerful stage presence. I knew it would take a long time, but I also couldn't say no to exploring every inch of the creative universe.

Because I had such a strong foundation from dancing, I know that part of the performance would be effortless. It was not a big deal to jump around while singing. As a dancer, controlling your breathing was as important as the steps. Dancing while singing was less effort than the full dance routines. I just slowed down the dancing a little so I could split my lung capacity between the words and the moves. I also controlled it by dividing the high-energy, dance-filled numbers up by talking to the crowd or DJing. That is probably one of the few times in my life where I felt totally free. There is a line in a Will Smith song that goes, "Life is a cage, but on stage I'm free." I have felt that every day of my life.

If you loved to dance, that was a great time to be a performer. Dance music and EDM (electronic dance music) showed up more and more on the pop charts. There were several clubs around the city that only played that style of music. I've always loved anything in that dance range of genres, and now it was on the main stage, not just small rooms around the city. At one point, I went to a club called Rock Jungle. This place held several thousand people and one of my favorite DJs, John Homan, from Metro Mix. It was around that time that I got the 5th gravitational push.

I started to learn a form of dancing that involved glow sticks. To be more precise, it was two glow sticks attached to two strings, and I flung them around with a sort of organized chaos. I not only loved this form of expression, but I also became very good at it quickly. I even made it the "big finale" to my live performances. Many times, along the way, I got the opportunity to judge glow stick competitions and perform demos. Still, to this day, I will have people say, "Hey, aren't you the glow stick guy." I feel I'm a lot more than that, but I usually just answer yes. It really was one of the most memorable times of my life.

I am now long removed from the days of dance battles and shows, but in a totally different way, dancing is still a giant part of my life. Almost each and every night that I'm out DJing, you can find me dancing in the DJ booth. To me, it's a very normal part of DJing. Keep in mind I'm not talking about mobile DJ gigs like weddings or birthday parties. These are bars and clubs that want you to entertain the crowd by mixing the music creatively. I think I do that well because I love to dance. If the music I'm playing doesn't make me want to dance, how can I expect the crowd to dance? The energy of the crowd is infectious.

You can't help but join in and experience that moment with them.

With this book, I hope to get you to embrace creativity. I try to look at how creativity is a root-level building block to everything we do each day. Some might say that dancing isn't creative but expressive. But what if the creative part is you creating self-happiness through the movements? You can look at dancing as the process of using outward movement to create inward happiness. To me, that formula has always worked, and I bet it would work for you as well. You just need to truly let go and dance like no one is watching.

I think everyone loves to dance even if they won't admit it. Some might say they don't, but that can be chalked up to normal insecurities. They feel inhibited by their danceability or afraid that others will make fun of them. It doesn't matter if you are a good dancer or not, you can still love dancing. There is a unique freedom when you forget about the world around you and just let your body move with the music. Dancing isn't limited by age, gender, race, religion, body size, intelligence, or any other way we humans feel the need to categorize ourselves. It's not even limited by whether you are standing or sitting. I don't care how old I get or what I can or can't do physically; I will never stop dancing, even if it's just in my mind.

Near the end of 2020, I hit a time that was both very, very sad and also very, very joyful. Sad because on December 16th, my former dance teacher, mentor, and long-time friend Joyce Darlene Ellis passed away after a long battle with cancer. Joyful because, like all the thousands and thousands of people whose lives were forever touched by her. I was extremely blessed to have had her help in the early days of my entertainment career and her constant encouragement throughout life. Besides dance, I took every type of class her studio offered, including acting, modeling, and speaking. She also gave me the opportunity to give back by being one of the boys' hip-hop class teachers. Beyond what we learned at her studio, she always taught us to believe in ourselves, trust God, and not chew gum in class (inside joke). She was a once-in-a-lifetime blessing from God to everyone who knew her. The Joyce Ellis Dancers were more than just people who I danced with; they were and still are family. Thank you, Joyce, for everything, and I'll see you on the other side.

Chapter 7
A Solo Symphony

Ask any DJ or musician why they do what they do, and almost every one of them will say something like, "music has always been a part of my life." Probably everyone who isn't a DJ or Musician will say the same thing as well. So, what makes it so different for a person who feels the need to spend hours working on individual note combinations or chord progressions? What drives someone to play or make the music that moves others instead of just listening to it on their own?

I think with me, some of that comes down to the way my brain works. I know you've heard me say many times that God made my brain different, but with most musicians, we hear notes and harmonies in things that aren't instruments or a song. We hear the music in everyday sounds around us. Windshield wipers, lawnmowers, construction equipment, birds, fluorescent lights all become notes and rhythms in the song of life. We hear when they join together to make a unique harmony and when they clash abrasively. We also hear how we would fix the sounds of life to re-harmonize and unite them. Life is one endless song because we hear music in everything.

When you're out in public, most people don't notice music playing in the background at every store. Part of the reason for that is psychological. Corporations spend a lot of money to keep you comfortable as you shop. If you are more relaxed, you will stay longer and spend more. There is a specific science to programming the music that reaches the customers on a subconscious level. The mind reacts to sounds on both conscious and subconscious levels. The subconscious reactions can even be measured on a chemical and electrical level in your brain.

Studies show that people tend to get stuck at the happiest point of their life when it comes to fashion and music. Retailers will use this to pull in and then keep a particular customer demographic. First, the music is tailored via the year or decade for the demographic shopping there. If it's a store where mainly younger people shop, you're going to have newer music. If it is a store with a broad general range of demographics, the music will reflect that. For the most part, you will find the music being played to be between 10 to 30 years old. The songs are chosen from that "average shopper's" happiest time in life when they were young and free.

Many times, songs are chosen that were written in specific keys because people react better to major keys than to minor keys. We tend to think differently when songs written in major keys are played. In a store or radio playlist, the songs themselves are even picked for rotation because of the time of year they were originally released. For example, if it's summertime, the songs on rotation probably came out in the summertime in that 10 to 30year-ago time frame.

Often it is chosen to help shoppers feel comfortable, shop longer and spend more. The music by genre and decade are selected to give a feeling of nostalgia. The songs themselves are chosen by both what key they are in, and the time of year they were released to provide the shopper with a happy, sentimental feeling. You hear a song, and you start thinking, "I remember when this came out." You might think about who you were dating or where you lived. You remember who you were friends with and the good times you used to have. Put all of that together, and you have something that most people don't even notice on a conscious level. To me, it stands out like a sore thumb. It becomes somewhat annoying because I know what they are trying to do, and it's working. It's also annoying because it is so predictable to the creative mind.

So, with that bit of explanation of what musicians or DJs hear beyond what most people can, you start to see why music has such an effect. I think that permeates the mind of a DJ or musician faster and louder than it does most other people. Partially because it's our job to know that stuff and because we think about it a lot more than most other people. The subconscious effect of music used as means of emotional manipulation will be covered in a future chapter. It is a massive part of any entertainer's job.

I grew up in a time where pretty much any new music you heard came from a radio station. Aside from that, our only other choices were records or cassette tapes that we probably learned about from the radio. The devices for taking pre-recorded music with you on the go only started getting smaller in my teens and early 20s. It wasn't a free and open field of music like now. Unless you had a compilation record, tape, or CD, you only got to listen to one artist at a time via an album. You couldn't just sample thousands of different styles to see what you liked best. The number of music genres is about the same as always, but there are WAY more sub-genres now.

The music industry was kind of forcing on you the music they wanted to sell you via the radio. As far as you knew, what you heard on the radio was pretty much all that existed in the world. There was no internet or any other way to catch new music. Unless you spent time in a record store or were part of a record pool, you only heard what the local stations played. I spend so much of my youth channel surfing every station on the dial to hear any and all genres. I think that constant search for new and different music fueled me to be a DJ. I also think it was that exposure to so many styles that gave me such a good ear for music.

I was just tuned into music on that subconscious level from such a young age. I remember a time when I was in a room with other people and a car commercial came on the TV. I said, "I really like the song in this commercial." Everyone in the room laughed and said, "it figures you would hear the song when the rest of us only saw the cool car." I know they were making fun of me, but the sad thing was they thought they were in tune with the world around them, yet they were actually missing so much. I understood the whole commercial. I saw the car, heard the music, and understood that the brand was trying to make an emotional connection between the person watching and how owning that car would make you feel. In real life, it's just a car, that's just a song, and you have just been tricked into believing the dream.

As a full-time DJ and reporter for Disc Jockey News, I make a trip each year to Atlantic City for the international DJ Expo. Keep in mind this is an entire expo of people who do what I do for a living. I thought they also took in music the way I did. One evening, I was walking down the boardwalk with a few other DJs. One of my DJ friends said he was amazed how I knew every song playing outside every storefront we walked past. I thought the other DJs knew them also, but apparently, I was playing my own game of "name that tune." As I would hear a song, I would say its name, the artist, and some other trivia about the song. I know my mind processes stuff differently, but I guess that was my mind's way of working through the onslaught of boardwalk sounds.

Apparently, I do the same thing when I'm DJing. Later on, that year, a long-time DJ friend stopped by one of the places I was mixing. As the night went on, we talked about the crowd and the music. Apparently, like before, I was talking my way through the mix. I was talking about the songs, how I would mix them, and the different breakpoints there were. At a certain point, he laughed and said, "It's amazing how you talk your way through each mix. It's very scientific or like it's written down in front of you." I kinda felt silly at that point because I didn't realize I was doing it, but like I said, that is the way my mind works through a hectic environment.

So, where does that leave me when it comes to the creative side of music? Some people only see music mathematically. It wouldn't be wrong to see it that way. The notes have a numerical worth assigned to them as they fit on the staff. Most modern dance music is built off a 4/4 time. That makes the combination of notes and measures very even, very balanced, and mostly predictable. Everything becomes modular to me at that point. Multiples of 4, arranged end to end, then overlap the present one's ending with the next one's beginning. You repeat this process song after song while adding different variables like scratching, blending, looping, and effects.

I see music piecing itself together like toy blocks. Some people only see the mathematical side, but to me, the math is already worked out. All I'm doing is putting the numbers in new creative orders. Find a key that matches, find a measure that fits, and create a way to make them blend together. Little did I know this mindset of mixing would play right into the next step of computerized music production that was coming to the home computer.

I first got introduced to making music on a computer called The Commodore VIC-20. At that time, it was mostly just digital sheet music. As far as I was concerned, from that day on, music and technology walked hand in hand. It just got better from there as computers became more powerful and more affordable. I started to flourish in the music-making and production side of things. Making music inside a DAW or Digital Audio Workstation was absolutely modular. I began to piece together beats and samples on a program called Samplitude. It came on a single floppy disk and cost around $300. It was just a basic multi-channel production program. Almost like a digital mixing board. Probably less powerful than many free apps you might already have on your phone right now.

That was during the big era of sampling. Taking parts from different songs and mixing them into a whole new one. I was able to deconstruct a song and put it back together to make something totally different or at least remix it to sound fresh and exciting. Besides my own sampling, I would buy pre-made, rights-free samples by the thousands in packs. I could make songs or remixes by taking drums from one song or sample, put it together with a different baseline, then a new melody, and so on and so forth.

Lyrics were the same way. I built a verse or a chorus or a bridge piece by piece. I put them all together like parts on an assembly line. When I was done, I had a completed song. That's still how I DJ to this day. I tear apart songs into different segments, find a place to mix them together live, and the party is started. It's that whole modular music mentality that just makes sense to me.

As DJ software got better, it made DJing more like live production. It was more than just putting two segments of songs together. You could also manipulate those segments with digital key changes, blending effects, filters, audio splitter, stems, or an endless parade of live samples. It truly was like live production on the fly. Some DJs hated it, but I loved it. I could DJ like I produce and produce like I DJ. Reading music waveforms have become a second language to me.

That is the process that my friend saw me talking my way through as I was DJing. When a song is coming to an end, I will pick another song in the same or near key. I manipulate it to blend with the same amount of energy. With the use of effects or tone knobs, I pull a little base out, highlight a kick from another song or soften the melody. I could create stutters and loops, finishing with an echo out, a fade-out, backspin, or drop. Then the mixing process starts all over again. To me, it's not difficult to look at music that way. What I have found challenging is explaining that whole "disassemble/reassemble" process to others. Some people only hear the song for what it is. They only understand it in its exact structural order. They can't imagine it torn into multiple pieces and layers. It doesn't make sense in parts, so they don't know what to do when it's in that state of being.

Unless you are a music person, all this might sound extremely confusing. I started to gravitate toward making music over making art because I couldn't turn up the art, but I could make the music as loud as I wanted. DJing was just a way to turn it up even louder. It was the art of live production. I could manipulate the music and the loudness on the fly in front of a live crowd. I could make it different every night. Controlling the music, working the sound, and manipulating the crowd's emotion was like moving in three dimensions at once.

Music-making hasn't stopped for me. I still make countless remixes and edits. I still make all the music that is in the background of my DJNTV videos. Just like many times before, where I am now is not the final destination. My journey is far from over. Without the lockdown, I'm not sure I would have realized that the fame and fortune that I chased was simply me looking for the next opportunity to be creative.

The creative process of making music has definitely changed along with technology, and so has how that music is consumed. With the invention of the "shuffle button," people began to accept music from entirely different genres being played back-to-back. No longer were you forced to listen to only one style of music until you changed the channel. With shuffle play, you would have a rock song followed by a rap song followed by some

Frank Sinatra. Anything goes for the most part, and I have to admit, I like it that way.

Creativity of all types is expressed and felt in the digital world without limits. Technology now gives us the options to be open and boundless with both listening to and playing music. It also provides the musician with a near-limitless sea of listeners for you to connect to. No matter what your musical voice is, you will find people around the world who, as they say, "are picking up what you are throwin' down." If you feel the need inside to express yourself, I promise you there are others out in the world who are on the exact same journey. The world may not always be positive, but you have the choice to absorb the negative and express it in a way that makes the world a brighter place. If you do that from the love of what you do, your light will shine, and it will illuminate someone's dark world.

Chapter 8
In The Mix

When I was in grade school, I remember using my grandmother's giant console record player to pretend I was a radio disc jockey. The idea that I could sit in a radio station studio and reach a sea of people with the music I played seemed like a really cool job. Little did I know then, but the radio business was not about the DJ sharing great music. It was about playing commercials and selling airtime. That part of a radio DJ's job is still the same, but so much else has changed. It once was a person who actually played the songs; now it's someone who just talks on the mic between songs. Some stations don't even have live DJs. All you will find at the station is a computer playing both the songs and a DJ's pre-recorded voice to make it sound like there was actually a live person at the station.

Growing up, TV shows like WKRP in Cincinnati made the life of a radio Disc Jockey seem glamorous. There was just something cool about getting a reaction from the music you played, even if the listener was riding in a car many miles away. You knew that you could make someone's day by playing their favorite song. Even cooler, to be the first DJ to play the next big song or artist before anyone else did. I bet it felt special to have the ability to give some artists their first break. It was very glamorous on the surface, but not always so in real life. It did have its perks, like the ability to get just about any concert ticket in town you wanted. That may have been the most glamorous side of the radio DJ, but there were other types of DJs. If radio wasn't your thing, you could be a Wedding DJ, a Party DJ, a Club DJ, or a Battle DJ.

I now make a living at being a bar or Club DJ, but that side of DJing wasn't even on my radar back then. I was either going to be a Radio DJ or a Battle DJ. At that time, those two worlds couldn't be further apart from each other. One paid you based on your speaking ability, and the other didn't pay a dime, but was all about your ability to scratch and mix. I remember watching bootleg VHS tapes of the early DMC battles with guys like DJ Cheese, DJ Joe Rodriguez, and DJ Cash Money. DJ battles weren't as well-known as they are now, but every DJ back then knew those guys were the kings.

Just like everything else, the DJ world has evolved. To stay in the business, you have to evolve along with it. The whole DJ journey for me has been extremely long. It was filled with moments of great creativity and complete sorrow. I once had someone ask me, "When did you know you wanted to be a DJ"? My answer now is the same as it was then, "I'm not sure I want to be one." I really never planned to be a DJ; it was always something I did to make money while I worked on being something else. Don't get me wrong, it is fun, and I find many parts like the technology and the on-the-spot creativity fascinating. All of that keeps me interested, but I never had some grand scheme and path to become a DJ, it just kinda happened.

Like most people who are drawn to DJing, I messed around with it for years before I thought I could make money at spinning. My first paid gig was in November 1987. My friend Bill and I got hired to DJ the local YMCA's Hawaiian Luau party. We put all our equipment and music together to be able to play in the big gymnasium. We didn't set the world on fire, but we did get paid. To be honest, I think we probably only made about $50 each. We may have taken the gig to make money that night, but we also really loved music. We loved how people reacted and danced. I really enjoyed playing the music and moving the crowd, but I believe most of that came from my love of dancing. If I knew what made me dance, I also knew what would make everyone else dance.

After that gig, live DJing started to really interest me, but the next big step was way off in the future. I was trying to go to college and work full time. Most of the gigs I did were smaller and very specialized. For almost a decade, I just had fun spinning whenever and wherever I could. I DJed for many Church events and small minor parties for years, but I didn't get my first real break until around 2000. There was a DJ company here in the city called Metro Mix. They were known for putting on some amazing weekly radio mix shows. I would record their mixes each weekend off the radio and then listen to them the whole next week. The music and style they spun really pressed all the right buttons with my love of music, dancing, and DJing.

Right around the year 2000, I got to know the owner of that company, John Hohman. He spun every weekend at an all EDM club called the Rock Jungle. That was during the era of the "super club," where thousands of people would gather under one roof to dance the night away. Rock Jungle was packed several nights a week with EDM fans grooving to John's style of spinning. Each week, I watched him spin and tried to learn mixing tricks or the hottest new dance tracks. He saw how much I loved DJing and music, so one day, he asked me if I would be interested in working for his company. There was a new club opening up called Matrix. It had four different rooms, each with a different style of music. Top 40, Trance, House, and Latin. John thought I would be an excellent fit for the Trance room.

Over the next few years, I not only got to spin several nights a week in Matrix but also got to spin in the other club Rock Jungle. I feel my time DJing at Matrix is where I grew the most as a DJ. It was also some of my fondest memories in all of my DJ career ... so far. I had so much fun and got to DJ the style of music I loved. During that time, I made friends with other great DJs and people who also loved dancing and dance music. I spun off and on at Matrix at least once a month until the day it closed in 2010.

During that time, I was also trying to make it as a vocal artist. As I got older, that part of my career was starting to die out. I ended up getting a day job and just DJed on the weekends. I really hated that day job more than I can explain, but it did pay very well. The funny thing is that God's timing for my life only had me at that job five years, and then I was laid off. Previously I was DJing once or twice on the weekends for fun or just some extra spending cash, but once I got laid off, I decided to try to make a go at DJing full time. That also meant I had to switch from spinning only dance music to spinning Top 40. I would say it took me a good 5 or 6 years to learn how to spin open format or Top40style music efficiently. It's just not my cup of tea, but where I lived, there was no way to make a full-time living playing only dance music. If you wanted to DJ full time, you had to be able to move the crowd with a wide range of music.

Fast forward many years, and I find myself today DJing 3 or 4 times a week on a regular basis. I also spin some specialty events, I'm the official DJ for a local sports team (The Pittsburgh Thunderbirds), and I get to spin at the international DJ Expo in Atlantic City. I've also been blessed to DJ and speak at DJ industry expos in Las Vegas and do the official debut video for Virtual DJ 2020 software. I get to see and be a part of so many different areas of the DJ business. I've been able to try so many different pieces of DJ hardware and try just about every DJ software. I believe getting to try all of that stuff helped me move forward when many other DJs got stuck in the "We've never done it that way before" mentality. Change is not only good; it's necessary. Dave Ortiz (one of the original employees of the company Zoo York) said, "Either you evolve with the times, or you dissolve with the times. You have to figure out how to keep going."

Now that you have the basic info on what got me to this point, the creative side of DJing is a whole different story. DJing on this new format of laptops, software, and hardware is worlds away from DJing the old way with records. I find the new way with the software gives me the ability to be creative on a multitude of levels. I am able to spin the sounds that I've always heard in my mind. I began to look at my DJing like I did my studio production or remixes. I was able to add live loops, effects, and many other things I once only could do in the studio. I now found myself doing studio tricks live in front of a crowd. I called it "live production," even though some DJs didn't like that definition. In their way of thinking, the two worlds were totally different. What used to take me hours in the studio on a multi-track software was now at my fingertips instantly manipulating songs in front of a live crowd every night, with just a laptop, software, and a controller.

It opened up an incredible mindset of how I could present songs, or even sections of songs, to the dance floor. Things really started to make sense to me in the mix. I began to put together different parts of songs like building blocks. I could build my dance floor piece by piece instead of just whole songs "as is." DJing started to become creative, not repetitive. My new creativity didn't stop with music. Software and hardware advances made it possible for me to also change or customize the tools of DJing.

Enter the world of MIDI mapping. MIDI stands for Musical Instrument Digital Interface. Basically, it's a programming language that lets the software speak to the hardware. It enables you to create an action for a button, key, or knob on a piece of hardware that changes or moves something within the software. Many electric piano keyboards utilize MIDI to make so many sounds come out of just one key. It may not sound like MIDI mapping was creative, but for me, I was building a world within a world.

My first experience with DJ software came in the early 2000s with a program called PCDJ. I didn't really get into MIDI mapping until the late 2000s when I discovered a program called Virtual DJ. With it, I could take a piece of hardware that was initially made to play a CD and make it work with a computer and software. I was creatively using MIDI mapping to repurpose hardware to work the way I wanted it to. From the hardware to the actual keys on the laptop, I mapped everything to make it work the way I wanted. Creative customization became a bit of an addiction. It wasn't till a few more years down the road that I figured out that I could pass that info on to other DJs through Disc Jockey News.

I then started thinking, why stop with just customizing the control functions? I should also customize the look of the software. Virtual DJ allowed me to change many aspects of the software, including its look, also known as the skin. I could change the placement or color of everything on the skin, including putting my logos in the spinning digital platters. Yes, it might seem a bit overkill to customize, but I did work in an industry where there was a lot of One-upmanship. This was the norm, and I was just getting started with my creativity.

In the world of DJing, my creativity gets to spread its wings in so many different ways. I'm not sure if my mind experiences DJing the way other DJ's minds do, but I know this way works very well for me. Beyond the DJ equipment, I also look at the "art of live DJing" slightly different from most. In early 2020, before the lockdown, I got to deliver a seminar in Las Vegas about basic mixing techniques. I talked about how my mind works through song choices. How different versions can take the energy and emotional levels up and down. How you can take a crowd on a bit of a side trip by playing something totally unexpected. I see what I do as a DJ and the crowd working together even if they don't. It is way more symbiotic than what is seen on the surface.

You just have to use all your creative tools to keep an audience engaged for the night. It is more than simply just playing a hit song. It's your job as a DJ to control the emotional level of everyone in the room. It's about unifying them and making them feel free enough to forget about the world around them. At least for a little while, forget about their jobs, their troubles, or even people standing next to them. You help them get lost in the moment. Or, as the Daft Punk song says, "Lose yourself to dance."

It is an absolute honor to work a crowd as a DJ to watch them shake away stress and worry or just have fun with their friends. I believe that to truly make that moment happen, you have to be in it also; you have to be having fun with them. I've had so many people come up to me and say things like, "You look so happy; you must really love what you do." Many other compliments happen all the time, but I don't take that as I'm the most skilled DJ; I feel I'm just lost in the same moment as the crowd, and that unity between us is tangible.

One time, I even had a girl walk up to me and say, "Do you have to be drunk to do this job?" I replied, "no, why?" She answered back, "because you look so happy and free, how do you do that without being drunk?" My answer was simple, "You guys are having fun, and so am I." As a DJ, I get paid to celebrate with people. I know that is a really basic description of my job, but I do get paid to celebrate with people. It could be celebrating a special day or just celebrating the end of a work week. If I can't enjoy celebrating with people, then I need to pick a different job.

When people talked about me looking happy or looking free, it took me a long time to understand what they actually saw. People can see if you are in the moment with them, they can see if your emotions are real. That is when everyone lets go of their crazy lives, lets go of their egos, and just dances, one beat at a time. Some of those nights in the booth helped me to understand who I was and what I was doing. I started to understand what made me dance and why that affected so many people to feel the need to walk up to a stranger and tell them how happy they were. I work very hard to grow my skills and abilities when it comes to mixing, but I found that it's so much more fulfilling to work towards uniting the crowd. To help them create a moment that they not only remember for years to come but continually want to find over and over.

That whole mindset took me back to a comment that another DJ made when I was spinning at the International DJ Expo. During that year's expo, I gave two different DJing demos. One was very intricate and required a lot of scratching and mixing. The other was kind of a free-for-all fun time. In my mind, the free-for-all was incredibly dull. To my surprise, most people commented they liked the free-for-all set better because it was "fun." I worked really hard and focused on the technical set. The other set didn't require as much concentration, so I jumped around and enjoyed myself. So did everyone else, apparently.

Again, that whole mindset took me many decades to understand. When I'm free and expressive, I'm still being creative when it comes to mixes and transitions. When I'm living in that moment, my soul speaks a type of creativity that is most beautiful and only understood by other souls on the same journey. It has a value that is hard to tabulate and sometimes even harder to recreate. There isn't a formula to achieve this or a map to guide you, but getting there is very simple. You have to let go of the "preferred" before you can receive the "priceless." All you need to do to begin that process is "Just Have Fun."

Chapter 9
Physical Versus Digital

Some people actually act as if there is a vast chasm between physical art and digital art. I've met many artists who shun the digital side with a persistent refusal. In this chapter, I hope to show you my journey from one to the other and how they both exist in perfect harmony today. They are not two different worlds, but the same world in different dimensions. They exist at the same time and have the same internal benefits. It stimulates the mind, strengthens your problem-solving skills, and reduces depression and anxiety. The best part is, in the end, it gives you something cool to display, show off and enjoy.

For me, most of my creativity started with drawing. I would spend hours upon hours just me and the paper. I would draw just about everything from futuristic cartoons to simple pictures of broken-down barns forgotten by time. In my early days, cartooning was the main focus. It was just a fun way to express myself without too many critics chiming in with their opinion. Cartoons left the creative box wide open. They didn't have too many boundaries or rules. For example, one of my favorites back then was a comic strip called "Bloom County." It had a talking penguin character called Opus T. Penguin. A talk penguin in a comic world is not all that odd. What made it seem over the top is when the artist flexed some creative license and granted Opus's desire to have cosmetic surgery (on more than one occasion) to get rid of his beak and replace it with a human nose. In a world full of rules, the cartoon world had very few, and it felt liberating.

I had a few cartoon characters of my own. One of them actually got kind of famous locally. Bonehead was his name and he was very close to my heart. He is the guy on the cover standing on the little prince's planet. He was kind of like a modern-day Charlie Brown. It all came about when a comedian in the 80s asked the question, "why is everyone on television skinny, rich, and good-looking?" I decided to put Bonehead in a TV-type world where everybody was exactly that, skinny, rich, and good-looking except for Bonehead and all his friends. They were imperfect in a perfect world.

Bonehead himself had many characteristics that were literal interpretations of insults. Take his name, Bonehead; he actually had a bone through his head. Just for the record, this was way before sideshow Mel on the Simpsons. Other literal characteristics were his negative eyes. Because the world around saw him as something negative, his pupils were white dots in a black eyeball instead of the standard white eyeball and black dot pupils. His friends were like him also when it came to their particular issues of one sort or another. For example, Bonehead had a friend called Spaz. This friend was lovely but a total spaz. Imagine an extremely frizzy pompom with a face. I felt that the literal interpretation of the insults made them hit home a little harder.

In contrast, the people on the other side were these extremely good-looking cartoon characters named Biffy and Buffy. Picture your typical 80s headband-wearing, tennis-playing rich kids. Just like in most cliché television shows, there were some characters that fit perfectly into both sides. It was all about social clicks and the never-ending struggle to fit in or be liked. It was very much a reflection of life in the world at that time. Even though I loved the free and open world of cartooning, I did see the real world as it was. It was cruel about stuff that was very surface and unimportant.

Besides Bonehead, I also had a few drawings that were random but noteworthy in the school newspaper and the school yearbook. I even had one of my cartoons picked for a national competition of all the Walden bookstores in the United States. Nothing ever came of that, but it was nice as a middle school age kid to have my drawing make it to the nationals. I often wonder what my drawing life would have been like in this digital age. The competitions would have been online, along with the comic strips I loved. Are kids today missing out on the fun of Silly Putty and Sunday color comics? I feel kind of lucky to have experienced both worlds in my lifetime.

There were so many different forms of art I was able to sample between my parents' store and the classes I took in school. As I have mentioned, I really enjoyed different styles of drawing. I loved everything from the wide-open world of cartooning to color pencil drawings or even just pen and ink. One of my favorites was scratch art. I think I liked its simplicity and how it's the reverse of pen and ink drawing. Instead of drawing a dark line with ink, you scratched away the dark area to make the area you want to be light. I also loved working with pastel chalks. There is just something about the warm colors and a vaguely blended line. I even spent some time diving deep into calligraphy. I think the only reason I tried it was an attempt to turn my horrible handwriting into some kind of art.

I did, and still do, enjoy photography. When I first got into it, there was no such thing as digital cameras. I spent a lot of time hands-on developing black and white film and creating prints. I've taken, developed, and printed both black and white and color film in 110, 35mm, 120, and disc film. I even got the chance to experiment with pinhole cameras back in the day. It's strange when you think about photography then and now. Then it was physical art, and now it's primarily digital. It's funny how things change like that. When I was a kid, phones had cords, and TVs didn't, now it's the opposite.

I didn't like all types of art, or should I say I didn't get into certain mediums. I didn't really like sculpting, even though I still have most of the sculptures I did. I've tried several types of clay sculpting, wood sculpting, and a few other mediums. I think one of the reasons I didn't enjoy them is how much space each project took up. Another form of art I tried but didn't stick with was screen printing. I loved creating patterns for t-shirts, but like the sculpture, it took up a lot of space that I never had to start with. I totally understand why artists strive to have a studio of their own, to have the freedom to just spread out and just create.

My mother was an outstanding tole painter. I gave that a try also, but again it wasn't something I really enjoyed. Like most people dabbling in art, I spent a lot of time messing around with watercolors as well. Over the years, I also worked with acrylics, oils, fabric, airbrush, and even a little graffiti. Painting was fine, but I just didn't enjoy it. I think it was finding the balance between working fast enough before the paint dried and wanting the paint to dry faster so I could be finished. Maybe that was just the impatience of my youth.

I even tried some of the applied arts by taking several drafting classes over the years. That would also fit into the "didn't enjoy" column because it was mostly about perfect lines. There wasn't much room for free creativity when designing a building to stand up and keep people safe. You always have to follow fundamental physics; what's the magic in that? No matter how cool it would look to draw a house that only had waterfalls as walls, it wouldn't work because a roof needs to be supported by something.

Thinking back now, I find it amazing that I got to try just about every kind of art or craft there was. Macrame, egg decorating, egg carving, miniature dioramas, toy making, needlepoint, felt art, decoupage, papier-mâché, pottery, ceramics, jewelry making, sand art, metal embossing, metalworking, leatherworking, woodworking, wood carving, and I think you get the point. Art is fun, and no matter if it's touchable or digital, creativity comes from the same place inside every creative person.

After spending most of my life doing some sort of physical art, life brought me a new medium called "digital art." One of the most attractive attributes of this new medium is that I never had to clean up after myself like the old way. No more cleaning brushes or putting away paints. No more covering drawings so they don't get messed up. No more putting pencils away or making sure the caps were on all the pens. I didn't have to worry about clay drying too fast or paint drying too slow. I didn't even have to worry about where I would store the art once it was finished. All I had to do was click save and then shut down whatever device I was working on.

It actually felt refreshing to not have your art lying around everywhere and the incredible ability to just pick it up anytime you wanted. As the technology advanced, a piece of art that I started on one device could be finished on another. Start your art project at home, then work on it while you are waiting for someone at the coffee shop or sitting on a park bench somewhere.

One of the coolest things was the mechanical side of this new process. Things like lines or shadowing could be more precise. Colors could be picked by a simple palette, not an endless sea of tones with useless random names. Or even better, you could use a sample tool and select an exact color from another section of that project or a totally different piece of artwork and use it right then. If there was a section that I didn't like, I didn't have to start from scratch. All I had to do was create a new layer to cover or replace that section or just click undo a hundred times and try again. This new medium also allowed me to send my art to anyone or post it for a multitude of people to see instantly.

Digital art did require you to have some sort of screen to view it. If you didn't, you could always either print it out yourself or send it to the local print shop and get a giant copy the same day. This new way of doing art made a lot of sense to the way my brain worked. It even let me embrace the fact that I loved mixing mediums like paint and ink drawing on the same canvas. Creating was just creating; there were no rules about what you should or shouldn't use. I could just make something look the way

I wanted it to look. I didn't have to worry about someone saying, "that's not real art" or "you can't mix mediums."

Little did I know years down the road, I would find this type of artwork as one of my favorite things to do. It was very peaceful for me to sit for hours making flyers for events or thumbnails for YouTube videos. It became a source of escape and serenity for me. A mouse, a keyboard, a computer, a monitor, and my headphones were all I needed. It was one of my happy places.

Like all other forms of creativity, technology grew and expanded to mobile devices. I found myself freely taking all the things that once were held in place by a stationary desktop computer and was able to run free on any digital device wherever I went. This digital form allowed me to edit photos, add fonts, adjust composition, or increase clarity instantly and with the power of the undo button. Many of the apps I used were absolutely free or only cost about as much as a single sketch pad did growing up. This new way of doing art felt like adding a rocket to a tricycle. It let my mind take what I saw inside my head and make it digital art in the real world. Create it on a digital screen and then make it into physical objects like t-shirts, stickers, and more, all at the touch of a button.

Physical art and digital art also worked together in the musical world. My DJ equipment and the cases it was carried in all got a stylized touch that was designed in the digital world. I could even self-create merchandise that I sold at my shows, like bookmarks, temporary tattoos, stickers, dog tags, headbands, t-shirts, and hats. It allowed me to create my own album art, promo packages, electronic press kids, web pages, and much more. The digital and the physical working together made so much sense, like there wasn't a separation between the two. They were both real and living to me.

The transition from physical to digital took a lot longer than it felt like it did. It seems like I have always been using the current technology, but the truth is some of the stuff I started on is multiple decades old. Some of the first programs were simple photo editing software. They didn't let you do a lot aside from changing the saturation or contrast of a picture, crop a photo, adjust its alignment, or reverse it, so it reads left to right. The older art programs like MS paint didn't let you do a lot either, but it still gave you the ability to create a drawing or manipulate something without worrying about ruining the original.

Some of that early 2D art quickly moved to 3D, especially in graphic letters. It wasn't long after that, but I was able to get my hands on legitimate editing software like CorelDraw and Adobe Photoshop. Almost as fast as the high-end software came, it got replaced by simple apps on a phone or tablet. They did about the same tasks but cost a fraction of the high-end programs.

The digital art tools that we have at our disposal now can effectively be put to use by someone who has little or no art training or experience. You may not be creating a masterpiece or something that thousands of people will see, but by using your finger on a touch screen, you can create something that someone will love, not to mention the enjoyment you get out of the process of creating. All of this is literally in your pocket and at your fingertips.

That simple process of creating in the digital realm stimulates the mind and helps you focus, and that lets your body de-stress. Anyone can attempt digital art because pretty much every tool or supply you need, you already have. You can create on a smartphone, a tablet, a laptop, a desktop, or whatever. All of those devices allow you access to countless free (or near-free) digital tools that can get your creative juices flowing.

There are also many apps that guide you along the way in creating art. They teach you how to sketch, set up the composition in a photograph or even draw a silly cartoon. There are art and drawing games out there that let you interact with other users on their phones across the world. It can be fun and a simple way to let your mind create in a protected environment while also connecting with someone else through the app. The digital world found a unique way to bring together both my right brain and my left brain. It gave them both a place to exist in and create from together.

The creative process can benefit you in many ways you don't realize. Like I mentioned before, making flyers and thumbnails in the studio with my headphones is a highly protected undertaking. It lets me work on both self-expression and problem-solving skills at the same time. It can reduce stress or anxiety, give me a sense of purpose and even a sense of accomplishment and pride. Creativity also encourages us to be lifelong learners, and that slows the aging process of the brain. It has been proven to reduce dementia, improve mental health by boosting your immune system. I'll be the first to tell you that creativity can help keep you young.

If you haven't been a creative person your whole life, you might feel a little lost when it comes to where to start. I can't imagine there is a wrong place to start. Try something, and if you don't like it, move on to something else. I always say, "To find what you want in life, you sometimes have to first eliminate all the things you don't want." Also, to help you get started and keep moving forward, there are endless blogs and videos that can help every step of the way. No matter what your skill level is, you will find someone out there with the information to guide you to the next level. No matter where your journey takes you, I promise you will love the journey and all the people you meet along the way. The first step is up to you; when will you take it?

Chapter 10
Lies and Manipulation

This may sound strange, but I personally believe that working in the entertainment business is one of the most manipulative jobs in the world. Pretty much any job in the entertainment world is built around manipulating feelings and emotions. Most of the time, the entertainer is hired to create an atmosphere or a memorable moment. That moment could be live with you in a large crowd or somewhere by yourself on a TV or in a song. It could touch a deep memory inside or just affect the point in time you are at right now. It could be something from your past or a wish for the future. Either way, it evokes a reaction from something that is only in your mind. Being an entertainer means you have to be good at lying to the crowd and manipulating them into a false reality to evoke the desired emotional reaction. The intentional distractions in the arts of magic and kabuki theater are specific and extreme examples of manipulating your mind for entertainment purposes.

This is also true for the job of DJ. There are a lot of diverse types of DJs; I'm known as a "mix DJ." Most of my gigs are in clubs or bars. My main job description is to mix the music in a way that everyone forgets what is going on around them and has fun. I don't spend a lot of time on a microphone interacting with the crowd. In fact, most places don't want the DJ to talk on the mic at all. I don't get out on the dance floor with the crowd and do line dances or anything like that. I'm hired to mix the music in a way that controls the crowd and keeps them engaged.

This means more than just playing hit songs. I have to be creative with the song choices and how I mix them. I have to decide if I should play the whole song or just play the hook. Do I play the plain radio version or surprise them with a crazy remix? I have to feel the movement of the crowd throughout the night. I have to take that feeling, then amplify it through a non-tangible emotional reverb. Through more mixing techniques, I extend or accentuate the mix as I transition between two songs. To make that work, I have to be attentive to the age of the crowd, where the physical building is located, and even how the people are dressed.

Throughout the entire night, I'm trying to evoke a roller coaster of emotions in the crowd. It might be an older song to bring back a nostalgic moment. It might be a line dance to unify the crowd in movement. It could be a song where people scream the lyrics at the top of their lungs. I might speed things up or slow them down. What a DJ is really trying to do is unify the crowd with each other through song, without them knowing it's happening. We are trying to get everyone to be in the same moment at the same time. When you achieve that, it's true magic … or is it just good manipulation?

Manipulation can take on many forms. They say life is what you make it. If that's so, then a lot of people's lives are just about themselves. Some might say, "I want to make everything positive or better for the world around me," but what they really mean is that they are trying to make things great for everyone else as long as it doesn't make things worse for themselves. Their actions may even be rooted in the thought, "as long as they are happy, they won't focus on me." I know that probably sounds terrible, but I promise you making yourself unhappy to make someone else happy will only last for a short time. Believe it or not, many people live their entire lives like that.

I've heard many men use the saying "happy wife, happy life." It may be just words to some people, but when a person really means it, that statement is both out of focus and really dark at the same time. It is essentially one person trying to keep the other happy so that they can be content themselves. It could even be both parties trying to make each other happy while counteracting the other's efforts. Either both parties are giving and caring evenly for each other, or there is a LOT of manipulation going on in that relationship. Trust me when I say I'm a guy, and I hear what guys say behind their wife's backs. There is also no doubt it happens vice versa. That type of relationship just doesn't work long term. The real gem of truth here is that no one can make someone else happy. We are in charge of our own happiness. If I constantly need someone to do something to keep me happy, I was never and will never "be happy."

They say that the average American lies to every 7th person they come across each day. You may say that is acceptable as long as no one is getting hurt, but living with that many lies is messy and complicated. With a bit of creativity, you can tell the truth in a constructive way. You can help them with what they are trying to achieve and convey that you care about them at the same time. I do know some people want to be lied to. They need their ego puffed up. That takes us back to one person always trying to make the other happy. That relationship can't and won't last long.

I know many people that are genuinely nice on the surface but are extremely angry and bitter people inside. Look at the suicide rate in the world. Look at both the numbers of people who have committed suicide and the number of people who have attempted it. Both of those numbers tell a story of people that live a life on the surface that seems quite "normal," but it's truly a different story from their point of view. I am by no means judging because sometimes in life, you do need to put on a brave face to get through a difficult situation. Either way, lying is a choice that alters someone's reality, and that does include living in your own false reality.

I've spent my whole life in the entertainment world, but I'm not a big fan of crowds. I often ask myself the question, If I say I'm not a people person yet I display exceptional people skills, is that a lie? Am I manipulating those around me to believe one thing when the opposite is the actual truth? I'm using my skills to get what I want. I want people to have a great time when I'm on stage. It's not that I want people to have a bad time, but how I make my paycheck is based on the crowd's level of enjoyment. If I got paid the same even if they had a terrible time, would I still work hard to be a better entertainer? If there was no downside to sucking as an entertainer, would I still work at bettering my craft? What makes me continue this act? Am I fooling them into believing that I like crowds to get a paycheck, or am I fooling myself that I don't like crowds to justify the times when I need to unplug? Whoa, that was too deep.

Let's look at some different ways people lie. It goes without saying that lying takes a lot of creativity. It also takes a good memory of what you said to who. A good salesperson or a politician has this down to a science. Kids knowingly lie to their parents, and parents openly lie to their children. A boss lies to his employees, the employees lie to each other, and so on and so on. I want to first focus on the negative types of lies that appear to be positive. Some might even say these types of lies are for the good of others. These are sometimes called little white lies. There was an old saying that went, "Put a little truth in every lie." Some people, including myself, would call that "spinning the truth." And that is one of the highest forms of creative manipulation. Shifting the blame is a form, and playing the victim is also a form. A lie by any other name is still a lie.

Lies and manipulation take on so many different forms that go beyond just spoken words. Studies say that almost 50% of people admit that they have lied on their resume or on a job application. Notice it says "admit," so that number could actually be much higher. Endless, and I do mean an endless number of people doctor social media photos. Edification is good, but it can quickly become just inflation of facts. I once heard someone say there is a difference between lying up, "I knew the answer to that but didn't want to say anything," and lying down, "I couldn't have done that because I'm not that smart."

That is sometimes referred to as word manipulation. It can be either the truth or a lie but how it's said determines how you intend someone else to see it, as something true or as a lie. All kinds of people use wording manipulation to get you to answer the way they want. They use nouns instead of verbs. For example, ask "How important is it to you to be a voter?" instead of "How important is it for you to vote?" They might use your name while talking to build a connection. Dale Carnegie, author of *How to Win Friends and Influence People*, said, "A person's name is to him or her the sweetest and most important sound in any language."

Many people consider advertising as manipulation propaganda. Edward Bernays, who was part of the tobacco industry after World War 2, once said, "We are governed, our minds are molded, our tastes formed, our ideas suggested, largely by men we have never heard of." Here are three methods of effective propaganda. Tell me if they sound like modern-day advertising. First "Mass Repetition." You see an image or words over and over till it works its way into your mind without you realizing it. The second is "False Esteem." Convince the person they are smart, that they have made the decision independently, and that decision will have conviction. Finally, number three "Emotional Association." If you can get the person to identify with something on an emotional level, they will believe it must be the right decision or the best idea.

Before I go any further, I don't believe any lies are positive. I also don't think I've ever met a person who agrees with me on that statement, but hey, it's my book. I can write whatever I want. When I talk about telling the truth, I'm not saying that you should tell the truth to be cruel. If you are telling the truth just to be cruel, then you aren't an honest person, you are a cruel person. You can choose words that are the truth, but also, kind or encouraging. Truth from a loving heart can build a bridge beyond words.

When someone asks you, "do I look good in this outfit?" you might say yes even if you don't think so. You may choose to lie to either avoid the conversation going any further, or you think your opinion will hurt their feelings. You might even detect that the other person wants you to lie and give them support. Lying can be a mutual, two-way street. If you change your wording from "yes" or "no" (a lie or the truth) to "you look fine." That statement is the truth yet did not hurt someone's feelings. Choosing to use the word "fine" does not mean you like it or hate it, you are just saying there is nothing wrong with it, and that is "fine" no matter what.

Lying and manipulation can be used as a form of survival mode. I'm not necessarily speaking of survival to save your life; I'm talking about people who have trouble dealing with the world around them. They use specific actions or words as coping mechanisms for survival. Some of it may not be actual lying or manipulation. It may be for things like steering a conversation in a direction that makes them feel less vulnerable. One of the most effective and well-used forms of this survival manipulation is deflecting the conversation. You can deflect it to shorten the conversation, focus on someone else, or simply change the subject. The creativity in this action is doing it so that the other person doesn't know the deflection is intentional. You make them think the subject change was their idea. A deflective Ninja can do this without even telling a lie. A well-executed deflection is unseen and gently nudges the conversation in another direction. Throwing a lie into that mix makes it less of a natural nudge and more of an intended ricochet.

An example of a skillful deflection is to control the conversation when someone asks, "Where do you live?" There are many ways to divert this topic. Most people just simply answer and accept whatever direction the conversation continues. A skilled deflector is going to know people might ask that question since it's a common one. The deflector might start before they are asked by saying, "It didn't take me very long to get here from (insert place)." Starting the conversation by giving information that you are willing to share puts the deflection power in your hands. You started the conversation on your terms, which usually leads to them talking about where they traveled from instead of asking more questions about you.

You can also give away more information than is asked. When asked, "where are you from?" I say, "I'm originally from (place), but I've been living in (place) for almost 20 years." Giving extra information affords me the position to ask the next question, "where are you from?" With that, I can deflect the conversation away from me for quite a while. If you give a little, you can ask a lot yet reveal nothing.

Another simple deflecting phrase would be, "I live on the South Side; where are you from?" This sort of statement reveals very little non-specific information but quickly deflects. Most people will take that question and tell you way more than you want to know. Or if you are really skilled or lucky, the other person may take the hint that you don't want to talk about yourself and take the conversation in a different direction themselves. Then again, you could always just use the blandest and stereotypical answers you can give. They might find you boring, and it might diminish the chance that there will be follow-up questions.

One-liners have always been some of my favorite conversation deflectors. These could be simple one-liner jokes to answer questions. When someone asks, "why are you still single"? I would simply say, "I don't know, just lucky, I guess." These one-liner deflections can also be quotes from movies. "What are you gonna do today?" "Whatever I feel like I wanna do. Gosh!" That was from Napoleon Dynamite, in case you live under a rock. Those kinds of quotes usually go off best if you can do a good enough impression of the person you are quoting. Character voices are one of my most used defense mechanisms. Or you can just go the super easy route and use a social media line and just say, "It's complicated."

Other forms of passive lying could be when you wait in your car until someone either leaves or shows up before you decide to enter a building. That's you manipulating the situation to fit your needs. How often do we wait to return someone's phone call or text message to better fit the way we want the day to happen? This type of manipulation could even go as far as baking cookies to sway someone's positive feeling when you have to ask them a delicate question.

Most people wouldn't count stuff like that as lies or manipulation. They might say that's just a normal part of life. As I mentioned before, my mind works a little differently than most people. In some situations, my mind works overtime trying to filter the world around me. It could be as simple as wearing headphones, so I don't have to hear people. I'm changing the actual environment to a way that I can handle. You probably wouldn't say that is lying, but what if I'm not listening to any music? What if the only reason I have the headphones on is so people will resist talking to me? Is that a lie?

Lies and manipulations come in so many forms. Some are positive and build others up, while some tear things apart like a bomb. Some are helpful, some are hurtful. Some are tools of attack and others are tools of defense. They might have names like positive reinforcement, sarcasm, or guilt trips and can be used against or for the people you love. If you choose to use these techniques, know that if done well, will involve a lot of creativity. To be proficient at this, you will have to imagine how different situations will play out and ad-lib on the fly. The creative mind can be an amazing tool to help or hurt. Just like actual tools in life, they can be used for good or bad. It may grant you a better life because they say ignorance is bliss, or you could wake up one day and realize you have been living a lie for years. It's ultimately up to you. The power is in your hands or, should I say, in your creativity.

Chapter 11
The Art Of People

I once saw a book titled *The Art of People*. Most of that book was about doing or saying things to influence others around you to react or behave the way you want; either influencing them in a personal way or in a business situation. My chapter on the art of people has nothing to do with that. It's not about influencing others intentionally but how our human bodies react or interact to create a very personal and unique visual narrative. Think of it as me observing different characteristics or actions in people around me and how they appear beautiful in an artistic way. For now, we will call them Outward Actions or "OAs."

These OAs can come from pretty much anyone at any time. It can be a sound, a color, a reaction, a mannerism, or any other countless thing the human brain projects in outward actions through the body. Many artists have waxed poetically about the human body. I get everything they are saying, but I want to talk about more than just the form. I want to talk about the things that are mostly unconscious actions that each human has. They can be hand gestures, eye expressions, voice inflections, body mannerisms, and more. They are the little things that give each person's character flair. They are the beautiful works of art that are human expressions.

We all understand the beauty of raw emotions that come from a photograph or painting. We all understand how our favorite song makes us feel. We are moved by amazing poetry or a great novel. The beauty that I see expressed is often missed by most people. It is the little things used in everyday communication with others or reactions to the world around us. It's what makes each of us unique. How we talk, our posture, the way we sit in a chair, or walk down the street. For most people, those things are not created or practiced. Their beginnings are formed at unknown points in our lives. Some of these OAs develop when we are very young. It's one of those little things that make us different from everyone else. After all, we are not mass-produced robots; we are art.

I've spent most of my life working in the sound world. I see the artistic side of noise. I don't just hear the volume or tone of a person's voice, but the inflections and the enunciations of each word. How the words are said is just as important as the words. Since I'm a visual thinker, someone's words become living murals that aren't easily forgotten. Don't get me wrong, not all of those murals are beautiful. More often, it falls into my category of "noise," not beautiful sounds. My definition of noise is simply a sound that I don't want to hear. My favorite song on a day I need silence becomes noise at that point. Here I want to talk about sounds that bring positive mental pictures.

Sound appreciation is very subjective to each person's ear. I've been told some people love the sound of my voice, yet others compare it to "Chinese water torture." In the music world, headphones are used by almost everyone at one point or another, yet you would be hard-pressed to find two people that agree which is the best sounding headphones. You must keep that example in mind as you read this chapter. The things I see, hear, or notice might not be beautiful to you, and vice versa. Like most things in life, it is subject to the individual. There is no more accurate statement than "beauty is in the eye of the beholder."

You might hear me say the noise someone makes is worse than the sound of my own bones breaking. I may say something smells so bad it makes me want to shoot a flamethrower up my nose. I might even say seeing someone do something makes me feel sad for the future of the human race. None of those opinions mean someone else liking each of those things is wrong or strange. In each area I discuss in this chapter, I hope to reveal examples that my mind finds in the world around me. Some days, I really have to search long and hard to find that beauty, but it is special when I do it. There is a subtle artistry I observe in my fellow humans that most people let pass by.

Since sound is such a big part of my world, let's start with it first. At least for me, when it comes to human voices, it goes way beyond simple accents. It could be something as small as the way someone hangs on to a single syllable of a word just a little longer that can make me smile or feel comforted. A well-spoken word can say much more than any regional dialect can begin to describe. The words can be simple, yet with proper conviction behind them, they can convey a bright and vivid narrative.

Take for example, the actress Jennifer Beals. I've always liked the sound of her voice. I could never really put my finger on exactly what it was that intrigued me about the way she spoke. Then one day, during an interview, she talked about how she grew up in Chicago, and like many who live there, she developed a typical Chicago accent. Some people made fun of how she talked, so at a very early age, she decided that she wanted to lose the accent. In the process of losing an accent, a person has to work on the speed of their speech and the timing of phrases or sentences. I think her deliberate attention to the syllables, sounds, and cadence of each word is what I like about her voice. It sounds like a well-played melody, harmonically in perfect time with each emotional expression. Simple, unintentional yet appearing as if choreographed by a master.

The tone of a person's voice can also be beautiful on its own. Lower-toned voices are seen as calming. That's not to say someone with a higher tone voice can't also be seen as artistic. A person can change the tone of their voice to suit a particular situation. In fact, many actors and actresses have worked character parts for years in a voice that's far away from their own. Their voice becomes an essential part of the character they are playing that seems effortless. If executed well, it often becomes hard to see the character and the actor as the same person. They almost become two different people that can never be in the same place at the same time.

There's a British sitcom called Keeping Up Appearances that I've always loved. On that show is a character named Daisy portrayed by Judy Cornwell. In real life, the tone of Judy's voice is actually low. She felt that her voice did not fit the character of Daisy, who was to be portrayed as an always smiling, full of life, child-bride type. Judy decided that Daisy's voice needed to be much higher and peppy. If you would have heard Daisy's voice before hearing Judy's actual voice, you could tell immediately that the octave switch was a perfect fit for the character. There is a certain beauty when an actor can create the perfect voice for a character that, until that time, was only a name on a script.

I guarantee that you have heard the voice of Peter Cullen more times than you can count, even if you don't know who he is. Peter has been acting since the 60s but is best known for creating the iconic voice of the famous transforming truck, Optimus Prime. In the late 80s, he got a call to voice a new character. When he went for the audition, all they would tell him is that they wanted a "monster sound." Peter asked, "what does the monster look like"? They said they couldn't show him because they didn't want the unique look of the monster to be leaked. Peter told them if I don't know what it looks like, I won't know what it sounds like. "I have to have something to relate to; I have to put myself inside it." After some discussion, they showed Peter a short clip from the movie, and he knew immediately how the Predator sounded. His creative mind imagined personality and expressions to a creature that never existed and technically never actually had a written line in the movie.

The voice is just one part of the complex human design. They say the eyes are the window to the soul. Just like real windows in a building, the eyes can be dressed to mask what is going on inside. Some people are exceptionally good at hiding their inner feelings. If you just take a moment and look, you can sometimes see the depths and lengths that some people have traveled. Some eyes are welcoming, others teasing, and still, some are as blank as they can be. There have been countless studies where participants were shown images of only someone's eyes and asked to guess the emotion that person was feeling. The percentage of correct guesses was extremely high.

That says a lot about the mind for viewing just one small facial feature and interpreting an entire emotion. Maybe we all need to take some time while talking with someone and actually notice their eyes to see if they could use a word of encouragement.

It wasn't until I started teaching classes in front of students that I realized how much I talked with my hands. When I watch videos of myself talking, I use my hands to express so much it looks like I'm a hummingbird trying to fly. The hands alone often can express more than just words. Politicians practice hand gestures to make voters feel comfortable and confident in their abilities. When some people talk, their hands seem to paint a visual picture in conjunction with their words. Comedians use gestures to make a joke feel larger than life. Even the lack of hand movements when talking can encourage the listener to focus on the words without distractions. Think about how universally a hand can convey stop, come towards, or even just move out of the way. Most people don't notice how much hands are involved in everyday anonymous communication.

An individual's mannerisms are as unique to them as fingerprints, yet some can imitate others to an uncanny level. It can be the hands, the eyes, the head, your shoulders, or just the way someone walks. Some people have the most amazing mannerisms. The way they carry themselves or how they move speaks volumes about their beauty. Most people don't even realize the gestures or mannerisms they express. To everyone else, they are often the things that draw us to them but seen from the inside, we can't see the beauty or hear the melody that our bodies mix into life.

Something as simple as a head tilt can express care or empathy that simply warms the heart. I used to know a lady that had one of those amazing head tilts. You could see that mannerism in candid pictures or just talking with her. The actor Warwick Davis played an Ewok named Wicket in "The Return of the Jedi." He had no actual speaking parts, and the costume he wore made facial expressions almost impossible. Warwick decided to give Wicket a simple yet very expressive head tilt that spoke volumes beyond the Ewok/Human language barrier. He even reprised the role in "The Rise of Skywalker" and made sure that even though Wicket was a little older, he still had that same signature head tilt.

When it comes to speaking, most people express themselves with a lot of words, sometimes way too many. Others only need a few words to make their case to the world. Yet fewer still speak volumes with no words at all. How often do we find our pillar of strength from a simple hug or shoulder to cry on? A nod or wink of encouragement can give you the confidence to keep trying. A smile to instill warmth or well-timed eye contact can reassure us that everything will be just fine.

Often the way we approach or greet someone will have a profound effect. Your posture and stride can speak that you are here for them in a time of need. The person might not know what you are going to say, but they know it will be edifying or encouraging. I used to volunteer at church summer camps with an older gentleman named John. Every time he would shake your hand with his right hand, he would slip a piece of candy into your shirt pocket with his left. People would often call him "The Candy Man."

It didn't matter if you would eat the candy or not; you felt that he genuinely cared for you. Still to this day, the thought of that tiny gesture has a massive and lasting positive effect on all who knew him.

Some of the most beautiful things in life take little or no effort. We don't have to change the world; just be empathetic to someone within arm's reach. You may not understand where someone has been or how they felt at their lowest point; you just have to remember what you felt like at your lowest point. The situations may be totally different, but the feeling is the same. My "struggle" may not be your "struggle," and your "struggle" may not be my "struggle," but my "struggle" is as big to me as your "struggle" is to you. You may not be able to see through someone else's eyes, but if you look deep inside yourself, you can remember how that feeling looked through your eyes.

The unplanned OAs of our personality appear almost choreographed to others. Just like some characters in movies or TV have "catch phrases" some people in life have catch OAs. It has even been suggested that body language and OAs can be more than 60% of our everyday communication. Now you know why I say some people are just "noise" to me while others are a symphony. Some mannerisms are seen as universal and used to read beyond what a person is willing to admit. Often, we try endlessly to hide what is going on inside, but one or many of our many body parts betray us repeatedly.

The betrayal of the eyes can come in the form of a long or short gaze. It can show you are interested and paying attention. On the other side, the constant breaking of eye contact can show that you are lying, that you are uncomfortable, or just simply distracted. Excessive blinking can show distress, or lack of blinking indicates you are trying to over-control the eyes. It says you have something you are concealing. One of the most revealing yet easily overlooked tells of the eyes are the pupils. Emotions can affect the size of the pupils as much as the environment can. In conjunction with the pupils, the eyelids and eyebrows work together to speak volumes you may wish to convey silently, or they can be your total undoing.

The mouth says just as much by its expressions as it does by the words it helps to form. You can clearly express many different emotions by simply biting the lower lip. There must be a thousand different ways a smile can convey every level of happiness, approval, anxiousness, confidence, smugness, mischievousness, or relief. That is only the "upside" of the mouth. The downside shows anger, sadness, fear, disappointment, disgust, disapproval, or unhappiness. Yawning isn't speaking, but it announces to the room a level of boredom that you may not want to be known. The whole face says so much that it leaves me with just one question, what does the "duck face" in all those selfies say?

I talked about how many other body parts communicate endlessly, but what about the distance we put between ourselves and others? Since this book was written during "social distancing," what does the personal space you require or create say when social distancing rules are removed? Edward T. Hall coined the phrase "Proxemics." It refers to the distance between people when they interact. That distance, in itself, can speak volumes. Hall defined four different distances in Proxemics. "Intimate

Distance" is 6 to 18 inches. It indicates a close relationship or comfort with the other person. "Personal Distance" is 1.5 to 4 feet. This distance usually indicates the other person is in the friends and family group and shows a level of built trust. "Social Distance" is 4 to 12 feet. This distance puts people inside the maximum personal communication area. It allows you to interact with people that you know or are meeting for the first time. It shows safety from or curiosity of those who are in that proximity. Finally, there is "Public Distance, 12 to 25 feet. This distance is usually reserved for public speaking, teaching, entertaining, or, in my case, I may be trying to avoid you.

The art of people is so complex to me. Sometimes it is overwhelming to attempt a level of honest communication with others. The complexity includes each person's willingness to share or to be truthful. It indicates our interest in interaction, the environment, and the level of trust. There are some social conduct guidelines, but they seem to be disappearing more and more as time goes on. That leaves us to step back and just appreciate the beauty of our fellow humans despite all the other factors. Sometimes you have to search very hard, but there is beauty and creative expression all around us. As the old saying goes, "There is good in everyone if you just look." We can still love the picture frame even if you don't like the picture?

Chapter 12
Pictures In Motion

We have all imagined stories in our minds. Daydreaming a scene, edit some actions to give us the outcome we wished would happen. Some might be positive, some not so much. Either way, we were telling a story to ourselves piece by piece. It was a mental video that we created. For most of my early life, imagining was all I could do. I didn't get to start with actual video recording until High School. At first, it was simply a way to just record a one-take video. Editing the videos wasn't easy back then unless you had costly equipment. As limited as it was, I knew from the beginning that creating with video, or at least some form of film, tape, or digital recording, was a powerful tool that I needed to learn and use.

Call me a nerd if you like, but yes, I did work in the AV center in school. I would run the video cameras for the different projects and later on even got to do some basic editing. Believe it or not, in the beginning, our school only had black and white reel-to-reel video recorders. They didn't get color video recording or VHS until I was almost a senior. During that time, I learned about video project management and storytelling in an art form other than still art. That little bit I learned in the AV center gave me so much to work with down the road. It was a priceless foundation for visual storytelling.

I talk a lot about this now, but when I was younger, one of my life goals was to have my own TV show. I imagined a comedy show like something Robin Williams did or a late-night talk show like David Letterman. At that time, a dream like that seemed so far away. If you didn't live near a major city, your only place to start was a public access channel in your town. I recorded and edited a few different shows and tried to get them on the public access station. The only problem was I lived over an hour outside the city, and you had to be a city resident before they would consider your show. The internet wasn't even on the map back then, let alone the ability to have a full studio available in our pockets everywhere we go. It's all there, camera, sound, editing, and distribution. It took a lot of different, expensive devices to make it all happen back then.

In the 90s, I watched the internet start to grow. I realized that in the future I wasn't going to need a TV station to make that dream come true; I was going to be able to achieve it using a new buzzword, "online." Seeing this come to an obtainable goal actually took much longer than I thought it would. Remember, YouTube didn't go live until May of 2005. Before YouTube was created, there were many small websites that let you broadcast or post videos online. Even at their best, they still didn't have near the audience you have with the smallest social media platform today. It at least gave me a place to create something and find an audience if I worked at it. I quickly learned that I could spend hours and hours performing or speaking on stage yet still not reach the amount of audience the internet gave me right from my home. As small as it was back then, it felt like the whole world was watching, even if only a few were.

Before good editing software became available, I tried to create any way that I could. Some of my first video edits were actually done with multiple VCR player/recorders. I would have one set to record the other one hooked up playing. I would record a section, then hit pause, take the VCR that was playing to the next section, let the pause up to start recording again. I did this over and over until I had the short video I wanted. Talk about doing whatever it took to make it. I just wanted to create videos that moved people. I wanted to inspire or encourage others. I wanted a bigger voice, and I knew video could make that happen. What it actually took was a combination of video, the internet, and mobile technology.

Andy Warhol once said, "In the future, everyone will be world famous for 15 minutes". Very early on, I saw things a little differently. I didn't think everyone would be world famous for 15 minutes; I figured everyone would be famous to 15 people around the world. With all of that foresight, the one thing I didn't see coming is how the smartphone would change everything. To this day, I'm still amazed at the powerful technology we carry around in our pockets. The high-quality video you can record, edit, and upload with a cellphone is a miracle compared to what we had back then. For example, my first handheld video camera wasn't actually handheld at all. It was so large you sat it on your shoulder like you were shooting a bazooka. They did get smaller as time passed, but the most significant change came when those cameras no longer used tapes. The digital age of media started to level the playing field. Instead of expensive equipment, all you really needed was a digital camera, a bit of creativity, and some time. Anyone with a digital camera and computer could take the video creation process from start to final production. All you needed then was a smartphone or computer you probably already had, and you were ready to produce.

One of the early video editing software was called Windows Movie Maker or WMM. If you don't remember, that was a free editing program that came with Windows and had some not so dazzling effects and transitions. It wasn't the best, but it definitely got the job done. Still to this day, I find videos on YouTube that have those WMM edits and overlays. We have much more sophisticated apps on our phones than what Movie Maker could do. Even though it wasn't much, programs like WMM gave us the ability to do what felt like magic.

I think one of the biggest advances came later. If you don't remember what it was like to render a digital video back then, computer speeds were much slower and took forever. You might have a two or three-minute video that took over an hour to render. Lord, have mercy if you found an error or mistake after your rendering was done. You had to build some good habits for checking and double-checking before you started the rendering process. Things did get better as computers got more powerful, and we did eventually get pro-level editing software, the ability to use green screens, and sophisticated graphics. I wouldn't trade the technology we have now for what we had back then but making videos with basically no technology helped me learn that all the fancy equipment in the world was no replacement for good creativity.

Video is where I got to use all the past creative lessons I've learned together in one place. There is a lot that goes into making even the smallest video. There is a mountain of work that goes into just developing the concept. Way before you worked out the logistics of your creation, you had to figure out how to sell the idea, and you had to be a good storyteller. My writing and public speaking classes helped with that. It also took storyboards, and those came from my drawing skills. You had to make everyone involved with the project feel the impact of something that was just an idea. Simple words, a well-told story, and some crude hand drawings went a long way to make the vision real.

Once you have everyone on board with your idea, it's time to develop an outline for the whole story. Try to use a visual flowchart to keep things in order. Those little details helped you get from the first idea to the final edit. I usually have 2 points in the story in mind before I start. I figure out where I want to start and how I want to end. Sometimes all I had was how I wanted it to end and a clear picture of what I had to work with. As we spoke before about Convergent Thinking and Divergent Thinking, this is where you use both of them to find the multiple ways to get from the beginning to the end. You then pick one or mix several paths together to create the journey you wish to take the viewer on. Make sure you have several anchors or pivot points along the storyline in case the reader or viewer needs to backtrack. Think of it as bread crumb markers to keep their attention on the next step so they won't look too far ahead and spoil the surprise ending you created.

Once you have the script written, you have to figure out who will play the parts or do the narration. Will the person you choose be able to make what you wrote believable? The best punchlines in the world have been ruined by bad timing or poor delivery. It may come down to the person editing the video that will make or break a project. There have been so many motion pictures saved in the editing room. Many times, the editor can even change the story entirely depending on how they edit. Some say they have more power telling the story than the person who wrote it in the first place.

Lighting a scene is one of the most overlooked yet crucial parts of the process. This is just my opinion, but good lighting is one of the hardest things to accomplish correctly in video. There are so many different ways to light a scene that will change the mood and focus without a single line being spoken. It can enhance the actor's delivery or totally wreck it. It can take the unbelievable and make it fact. Even if it's a simple "talking head" video, having the proper lighting and background can set the mood that will either draw the viewer in or make them tune out. When it comes to lighting and sets, don't be afraid to ask for help. Both areas take years to master and are fine arts in their own right.

Once you start filming or recording, be prepared for anything. So many variables can come into play at this point. It can be something as simple as a glitch with equipment, the weather, human error, or most likely human emotions that can derail an entire day's filming. If I were to give you a few words of encouragement for this stage of the project, it would be, "Stay focused and be flexible." The more you prepare, the better you will be, but also leave room for unexpected creativity to bring you some beautiful and priceless gems. The show Parks and Recreation would allow 5 minutes at the end of each scene shoot called "fun runs." This is where they would roll through the scene quickly and let the actors ad-lib what they felt worked best. You would be surprised how many of those unscripted moments became the funniest points in the show.

Before you start the editing process, there are a few things left to think about. First is the soundtrack. I once saw an online video about making hot cocoa done with the most ominous music. The music made it seem like the person was preparing for war, not making hot chocolate with marshmallows. It was funny, but it shows how each part of the creative world will enhance another if done well. Think what your favorite scary movie would be like without the dark and threatening soundtrack. That's also why some TV shows are filmed in front of a live audience; to get the crowd's natural reaction instead of just canned laughter.

One of the last things you need before editing is the establishing shots or product shots. These are short videos that show the outside of a building to "establish" where the next scene occurs. The product shot is simply a well-lit picture or video showcasing what the video is about. Both give the viewer a baseline of what will come next. Even though these are videos, I like to set them up like a photograph. I make them have a distinct point of focus the viewer can easily understand. Make that clip tell a story like a narrator speaking directly to the audience. These shots can pivot the story on a dime and cement it as the foundation of what will follow.

All of this is mainly for "long-form" videos. Even though your video may be just a few minutes, it is an eternity longer than some platforms that only allow videos 15 seconds or shorter. These micro short-form videos make up a lot of the average viewers' content intake. Some might not consider them serious art, but they let the creator flex their creative muscle daily. Many creators have built their entire careers off these micro short-form videos. To some, they may seem pointless, but there is no denying the popularity. It is a worldwide phenomenon that can launch a career or get you the next gig.

Speaking of posting your videos online, there are boundless amounts of creativity that go into just posting videos to maximize viewer count and impact. You have to post at the right time with a catchy title and the right thumbnail. Those three things can make or break the full reach potential of a video. On some platforms, a creator can benefit heavily from the right hashtags. Some of those simple steps done with creativity can take a video and its creator to a whole new level. You can either do this stuff yourself or hire someone. Either way, I cannot emphasize how crucial creative posting is to an unknown or growing artist. You may think of it as a minor action, but even if it connects you with your current audience or builds on that, it is a very important skill.

Most people don't see beyond the art itself. They see an artist painting a picture and find enjoyment in how it looks or makes them feel. Rarely do they think about the skill and knowledge in choosing the right paints, the right colors, and the right brushes. Most don't think about the proper pressure or angle needed in each brushstroke. A truly skillful artist can blend the colors on the canvas in a way that takes the painting beyond just a few thousand brush strokes; they can make the artwork come alive. The creative process in creating a video is the same. I often use every aspect of my creativity. I dip my creative brush into skills and knowledge I've picked up from drawing, photography, painting, sound engineering, writing, storytelling, editing, and stage performances. Not to mention the creativity that it takes to make a project stand out in a sea of others screaming for attention. You have truly succeeded when people not only see your art and vision but become invested in its existence. They become emotionally invested in every part of the creation, even to the point of mourning it when it's gone.

With today's technology, anyone can record, edit, and present their cinematic dream. From special effects to a killer soundtrack, you have all the tools in your pocket. The only thing that might be missing is that you haven't allowed yourself to dream it. Take an hour out of your day this week and let your mind dream in detail about a project you put on the shelf for whatever reason. Today's dream will pass when today ends, but the dream doesn't die today. It lives in your imagination every day you are alive.

Most of the stuff I talk about in this book is looking past something in its finished form. A completed creation isn't a final product to me. It seems more like just one step in the long line of creative stages. Finishing one project just gives you the opportunity to start creating another. You begin moving forward on the next project because "next" is the only option to a creative mind. We have the ability to both stop in the moment and move as it grows. A stationary point really isn't fixed; it just passes at a slower speed than most might be able to see. Don't be fooled; it will always pass you by unless you are moving with it at its speed. Either way, the journey continues, just like each frame of a movie passes by the lens to make it come to life. Don't forget to enjoy this frame of the movie but also look forward to creating the next frame.

Chapter 13
Words And Words

My mother once said, "if you can read, you can learn to do anything." There have been many times in my life where I was so glad that I learned to read and that she helped me see its lifelong value. Like most people, I spend a lot of my life dealing with words. It can be anything from putting them together to convey helpful information or encouragement to just talking to myself. Rarely do I ever fear writing or speaking, but it's not always been that way. For many years of my early life, I did whatever it took not to be noticed. That meant even though I did write, I didn't share it with anyone. Not to mention that public speaking was probably the most dreaded thing I could imagine. I never raise my hand to answer a question in class and definitely didn't strike up a conversation with strangers. I only spoke up in public when I was either forced to or as a defense mechanism to blend in.

I wrote a few odd stories and poems when I was young. Looking back, I didn't realize how much I enjoyed writing. Until recently, I would have never picked it out as important from all the creative things I do. Thinking back, it really surprised me that out of the blue, I decided to take a journalism class in high school. It wasn't a required class, and I didn't think of myself as a writer, but I really wanted to learn more about that world. I wasn't thinking about being a writer or anything. I don't even remember why I took the class other than I just wanted to know more about the journalism world. Surprisingly, I enjoyed building narratives in short form. I think that class helped me learn to be a better storyteller and to express myself.

It showed me how to get an idea across quickly and how to choose the right words to get someone's attention.

It was a small class, less than ten people, if I remember. Like I mentioned, I didn't raise my hand or participate much during any of my classes, but journalism was probably one of the only places I actively engaged with the teacher and other students once I crossed a line in the sand. It was early in the semester when the teacher asked me what I thought about a subject. I said, "Oh, I really don't have an opinion." The teacher came back with something like, "You have opinions like anyone else; go ahead and give it." I think that's all it took to get me started. One person telling me it was ok to have my own thoughts, and more importantly, it was ok if those thoughts were different. I'm not sure why that resonated with me so much, but that's all it took to express myself on a new level.

Before that, a perfect example of me writing creatively (but not wanting to draw any attention to myself) happened during an assignment in psychology class. The teacher hung a picture of a ship in the front of the room. The kind of ship you might see in a pirate movie. A huge galleon with large billowy sales that were very seaworthy, no matter the conditions. The assignment was to write a short story that went with the picture. Whatever we imagined was happening on or around that ship, we were permitted to embellish with wild detail or leave vague for the reader to complete. To encourage us to write freely, the teacher said if we wanted to remain anonymous, we didn't have to sign our name to what we wrote.

My story was a simple one yet very cliché. It was probably already floating around in my head from some other story I read or a movie I previously watched. Here is a brief summary of that story. It began with a sailor by the name of Captain Jack. Yes, Captain Jack. This was decades before the Pirates of the Caribbean movies. Captain Jack and his ship were out on the ocean, living life by their terms. One night, a storm came out of nowhere and threw the ship back and forth. Captain Jack did his best to right the vessel, but the last thing he remembered was a giant wave hitting the side and tossing him overboard. The next thing he remembered was waking up on the beach. His ship was nowhere to be found; no crew and no other land was in sight. Captain Jack spent a very long time stranded on that island. He did the best he could to survive, but it eventually became too hard. One day, when he was near death and about to give up hope, he glanced up, and right in front of him bobbing aimlessly and carelessly near shore was his ship. It was as if it heard his cry of desperation and floated back to rescue him.

The teacher said he liked it very much and that the ship returning shows whoever wrote this had a very romantic streak in them. He allowed the writer to speak up and share their vision for what they wrote. For the sake of avoiding attention, even for positive comments, I decided to stay silent. I felt it was best to just let my work speak for itself. To this day, I still choose many times not to explain or defend my work. What I create can and will stand on its own. I will speak up if it's necessary, but for the most part, whatever you get out of my creativity is fine with me, even if it's different from everyone else's.

After that, I wrote some other short stories for fun. I also spent a lot of time writing skits and plays for churches and summer camps. Looking back, those times aren't my fondest memories even though I received a lot of "quiet judgment." You would be surprised who can hear you talk even if you whisper. They would use words like "weird" or "artsy." Part of them probably meant that as some hidden compliment, but I knew what they were saying "big picture, "I was different. To me, why point that out? They were different from me, and I accepted them. They all had things that I could have pointed out and made fun of but chose not to. Different is neither bad nor good; it's just … different. Remove labels like that, and different becomes the best of things.

Words are VERY powerful for the positive and the negative. They can destroy with vindictive selfishness or build back up once you have understanding and empathy. I chose not to retaliate insults with insults. Revenge may feel good, but it is a total waste of energy. Whenever those situations cropped up, I would just say to myself, "keep moving forward." As a running back in football, one of your best tools or skills for making it to the end zone is to keep your feet moving, and that's just what I did.

After my college years, I started to find power in my writing and speaking ability. For some reason, people were willing to listen. Maybe it was the novelty factor of me being different, or maybe I really had something they wanted to hear. Even though I did an extreme amount of writing in college, that stuff was far from creative or expressive. It was a nearly robotic production of speeches or papers to get a good grade. I found with the things I worked on after college, I could have much more artistic freedom. I could take the listener or reader in whatever direction I wanted to, and it wouldn't be called wrong.

During this next period of my life, most of my writing was song lyrics. It is a departure from the traditional type of writing, but it is still writing, still creative, and very expressive. As I speak of many times in this book, the skills learned from one area help another. The lessons learned in high school and college classes differed from writing songs, but without a doubt, they helped in this form of creativity. Songwriting was an amazing expressive outlet, but it would be many years down the road till I returned to the traditional types of writing.

This time was just like many other times in my life, where I finished one type of creativity and quickly wanted to move on to another. I had released my final album, and without knowing it, I started to look for another outlet. I was approached by a DJ website to write an article about something in the DJ business. That one article turned out to be seventeen articles. I covered everything from hearing loss in the music business to finding creativity during a dry spell. They were really great outlets of expression. Notice how I don't talk about them as "they were good articles to read" but as an excellent way to imagine, create and express. They must have been worth something to someone because all 17 were re-published by Disc Jockey News many years later.

My time with Disc Jockey News is where my writing and speaking started to get much more refined. I wrote articles for the magazine, scripts for voice-overs, and bullet-point lists for live and recorded videos. The videos were not great masterpieces by any means; they just explained how something was done or information on a new product. Little did I know how much people would like them and how much they would help me grow as a writer and presenter. I was told by another video company that they used my videos as examples to their presenters on how they wanted their company's videos to be done.

I even got the opportunity to write scripts and do voice-overs for radio commercials, corporate videos, show intros, and DJ intros. It wasn't the most creative or dazzling work I've ever done, but the people liked it, and I got paid. The money was nice, but even then, it wasn't even the motivating factor. I was getting to be creative with my words in so many different ways. It was starting to keep pace with my DJ work. I always say I would rather be the DJ than teach the DJ, but sometimes you are what your paycheck says you are. I guess that gets us close to where this book comes in.

I've had several people (in a mocking way) say they were going to write a book about me. I knew they really didn't intend to write about me; that was just their way of saying I was so different someone should write it down. I admit I've always had an interest in writing a book. Many times in my life, I've drawn outlines and idealists about different topics. Somewhere I even have a whole list of book titles and possible topics. It took a pandemic lockdown to realize that I actually had something to say and the confidence to say it.

Remembering that one Sunday night, while watching the show "Making It," I found myself thinking of all the things I've done over the years. I looked at all the different areas that I was creative in and how those areas overlapped each other many times. As I thought about all the different ways I used creativity in my life, I went from saying things like "no one would want to hear what I have to say" to writing down a VERY long list of things I've done in my life. Sitting in that chair, taking note after note, I saw chapter after chapter covering topic after topic start to come to life. They all just fell into place effortlessly, like they all knew where they belonged. It was like the words were already written; they just needed to be let out.

Once I realized my motivation for chasing "the dream" all these years was just to be creative, I looked at my life in a whole different light. In metaphorical terms, I've already sailed "all the seven seas" of creativity. I've visited almost every country of expression and imagined along with people from every land. I've made pictures from scratch, photographs, and videos. I've made sounds with instruments, computers, and my voice. I've shaped, modeled, and applied art supplies of every type in every medium, and I assembled words on paper, on the air, and in person. I really had done a lot more than I gave myself credit for.

When I looked up from writing that list, more than two hours had passed. I looked at the list of topics and realized how much I really had to say. I wondered if I would be able to break down each of these areas and describe what I did and the creative process. Was I going to be able to take all the pieces of information and twist them into an entertaining tale that inspires others to keep moving forward? I wasn't sure, but I knew this was such a unique time of life. Being in lockdown afforded me an opportunity I would probably never get again. I had to take a chance and step forward with this project. I'll admit, at times during the writing and editing process, that confidence diminished. I kept thinking, why would anyone want to read my words about creativity? My answer to that was I couldn't stop writing. I couldn't keep myself from expressing those thoughts and ideas. My creativity about creativity was alive.

As days and weeks passed, I found myself writing constantly. I began to expand on ideas I had already noted. I didn't know how much time I had to do all of this. No one knew when they were going to lift the lockdown. Can I get all of this done before I have to go back to my busy life? The only thing I knew was I had to keep moving forward. I had to find the words no matter how far I had to go to get them. I just wondered if I was willing to go down some of the roads in my past. If I did, would I make it back the same?

I'm a firm believer in listening to your gut. Your first instinct is usually right. There are so many times in life I second-guessed my gut feeling. Some of those times were just to give something a try. I hate "what ifs." So many times, I would go through an experience, against my first instinct, just to get rid of the "what if I didn't give it a try" question. Those kinds of questions can haunt you for years. There is nothing wrong with doing that. I've said this before, to find what you want in life, you sometimes have to first eliminate all the things you don't want. With that said, you really do have to trust your gut. This entire chapter is about you writing and speaking, and since a lot of conversations we have are inner dialogue, you also have to listen to yourself. Can you receive your own words without filtering them? No one can hear what we say to ourselves. Would you be ok with others hearing your inner self-criticisms and comments? Would you let others talk to you if they used your own words? To be a good writer or speaker, you have to listen to yourself and the world around you. You have to let life speak without interrupting. They say life is stranger than fiction, so stand aside and let life spin its tale.

Being a good listener says more about you than your words do. I have been thanked for my great advice at the end of some lengthy conversations where all I really did was listen and say "Ok," "I understand," and "really." When it comes from the heart, some single words tell their own story. Just like a couple of words can speak volumes, some short two-word sentences like "I understand" can be all anyone needs to hear. I picked up a two-word sentence a few years ago that can be used in so many different situations. More importantly, it conveys a depth of care and understanding. If you have a friend or stranger pour out their hurt about something they are going through and you don't know what to say, try saying these simple two words of empathy and compassion … "that sucks." The statement affirms the truth; it is empathetic because you feel their pain, but it isn't advice or some lame platitude. You are just joining them in solidarity. You are basically saying, I hear you, and I'm here for you.

When it comes down to it, writing and speaking may be the primary ways to convey things from your point of view but don't forget you have others. Even if it's an instructional manual on how to assemble a bookshelf, you still imagine the steps you would take to finish the task. Take some extra time to evaluate your thoughts and your words. Think about what you actually say and don't say. You can't go through life expecting others to just "know what you mean." Say what you mean and mean what you say. Others take you for your words as much as you take them for theirs. Writing can be one of the most therapeutic forms of creativity. You start with what is deep inside, what no one else can see or hear. You take that and mold it into what you want them to hear. It can be the whole truth, part of the truth, or a total lie. Either way, they are your words to the world; choose them wisely. What story will be remembered, the one you tell yourself, the one you tell others, or the one you create that ends up being your legacy? I would encourage you to be honest yet understanding. Hear your own words and hear the words of those who are near you. We don't have a bionic hearing because God only intended us to listen to those who are close to us.

Chapter 14
Creativity Is Everywhere

Sherlock Holmes was a master at the art of observation. He noticed everything down to the smallest detail. I know the level of attention that my brain functions on, so I couldn't even imagine going through life inside his head. He could see the good and bad in everything around him, as if they were words on a page. He would not only notice people but also the state of everyday objects. You might see just a bridge; he sees the bridge and sees the cracks in it. He starts to put that information together with past knowledge he has acquired about structural integrity and its decay over time. He begins to process the number of people and cars crossing it each day and what is likely to cross in the time it takes him to get from one side to the other. True, there are always variables, but as Mr. Holmes says, "Paranoia is the byproduct of being consistently right."

The world around us is in a constant state of decay and creation. As the old passes, the new begins. I won't lie, there are a lot of not so beautiful things and some really ugly personalities in the world. Some days one is hard-pressed to find something worth smiling about. If you take the time and effort, you can find some brilliants in life's mess. It may even take complete darkness to reveal tiny points of creative light. You don't have to paint the next masterpiece or be the next great actor to be creative; it's all around us in everyday things. We walk by so much creativity in the ordinary. We miss some pretty beautiful things in the name of "schedules." Some are man-made, some are all-natural, but both have boundless hidden creativity and expression. Sometimes you have to give yourself permission to stop and look around.

When the novelty of life wears off, you forget there is still so much yet to see. As an adult, I get annoyed by bugs, yet when I was a kid, seeing a dragonfly or a lightning bug was awesome. It was the newness of the world around me that had me in awe. Birds, animals, and insects show a repeating circle of creation by nature. Other things in the world can be just as beautiful and wondrous as the most exquisite paintings or complex symphonies. Those marvels of life may be right next to you but aren't always obvious. To find them, you have to just stop moving forward so fast. Most of the time, you only need to shift a little one way or another for a new perspective. Look at something in a new light, and you just might see something different but also remarkable in its difference. Most people don't notice a lot around them because the speed of life is ever increasing. One of my favorite lines from the movie The Shawshank Redemption was when Brooks Hatlen saw the outside world after being behind bars for 50 years; he said, "The world went and got itself in a big darn hurry." That was the perspective of a man in 1955. I wonder what Brooks would think about the world today.

If you allow yourself just a few minutes every once in a while, you will be amazed at how slowing your mind to the speed of nature can show common threads between everything. To me, the waves at the ocean sound like all of nature is breathing in and out calmly. Consciously slowing down your breathing to the pace of the waves will permit your mind to get out of tunnel vision mode and notice what you have been taking for granted. Take the sky, for example. People rarely look up and notice the sky anymore. I love to look at clouds. Where I live, you see a lot of them. Even as an adult, I love to let my mind create images from different shapes. As one passes, the canvas is cleared for the next shape to transform into a living likeness. The creative person sees art even in everyday things.

When I see trees or tall grass swaying in the breeze, it makes me think of the master painter sweeping his brush across the canvas of earth. Sometimes that canvas is as large as the stars in the universe, while other times it's as small as the universe under a microscope. In the modern age of technology, via the internet, we get to see so much that only a few saw in the past. Inventions like the Hubble telescope let us see beyond countable time. In 2015, we got to see high-definition footage of the planet Pluto via the LORRI telescope aboard the New Horizons spacecraft that was launched nine and a half years earlier. I'm not sure which is more impressive, the journey to and photos of Pluto or the fact that anyone on the planet could view an event at the edge of our solar system live on their cell phone.

If we go the other direction and look at the small universe below us, we will be just as astounded. The transmission electron microscope lets us view something as small as hydrocarbon chains move across a graphene surface. We get to see a universe below us, just as big as the one above us. Electron Microscope photos and videos are amazing. Each year, Nikon holds the small world motion photomicrography competition. These are videos of everyday life around us that are too small to see with the human eye. It is mind-boggling to see a creature that is 0.5 mm, like the Tardigrade, moving and living in real-time.

You don't need a telescope or microscope to see surprising creations all around you. There are wondrous things created and expressed by other humans that might be next to you right now. Everyday objects or people doing ordinary things observed with a curious mind will seem like magic. Momentarily change your inner perspective, and things come alive. Growing up, I was a big fan of the David Letterman show. He had a recurring segment called "Stupid Human Tricks." These were everyday people with remarkable talents that basically had no practical use but were fun to watch. In a way, they were their own art form. Since this was before the internet, his show was the only place you could watch them.

Fast forward, and the internet gives us a window to the good and the bad. We can watch atrocities unfold in real-time, but we can also see the very best from our fellow humans. It can give us a first-hand view of people and things from around the world that you would have never heard about 20 or 30 years ago. If you want to spend a few fun minutes and see human action in artistic beauty, just search YouTube for videos about "amazing people" or "workers with amazing skills." You will see people doing everyday jobs and tasks, some you might do yourself, in truly mind-blowing ways. Some humans can take mundane tasks and make them complete works of art. There might be things around you right now that were created with incredible and surprising talent, yet you see them as everyday objects.

Besides the tasks humans can do, look at the things humans have built. Think about some of the man-made structures you have seen made for just living in or standing on. There are so many houses, communities, businesses, resorts, and destinations around the world that don't even seem real. There are places on this planet where humans have made new land where once only water stood before. Island communities built on man-made land in the ocean, on swamps, or over reclaimed garbage dumps. The size of these projects can be simple and small or so large you couldn't imagine it wasn't always a part of the landscape. There is a major airport in Japan called the Kansai International Airport. The entire airport, its runways, buildings, and onsite transportation were built on an artificial island in the middle of Osaka Bay.

In contrast to the sheer size of islands, the intricate integration of features that are a part of some tiny houses makes them feel like you are walking into a magic wardrobe. With an entire living-space less than 400 square feet, some tiny homes have all the amenities of a house much larger. Some impressive engineering has gone into those living spaces. It not only has to be functional, but it also has to be livable and comfortable. Most of them are also mobile, so if you don't like your neighbors, just hook up the house to a truck and find a new place to live. The term "minimalism" was made popular in art and music during the 1950s and 1960s, but the idea of minimalism goes as far back as Buddhist monks. That mindset changed to "bigger is better," so enter the industrial age and the power it gave us to expand in all directions.

Without a doubt, the machines man has built made most of these things possible. Consider the largest rockets and space stations above us or the gargantuan excavators and dump trucks on construction sites. Without those machines, the world would look a lot different from the ground or from space. Without the large machines, we wouldn't have GPS or Google maps, and now we know exactly where we are at all times. We wouldn't have many structures like the islands mentioned above. We wouldn't have many of the buildings we work in, play in, or visit as tourists. We wouldn't have cars at an affordable price, electronics from around the world, and 30-ounce soft drinks for under two bucks.

As impressive as these things are, most of the creations or expressions I want to point out would fall under the everyday overlooked category. Consider roads, sidewalks, and parking lots. They serve an obvious purpose, but they are built with so many hidden and needed attributes. Before the builder starts, they have to consider the water flow direction on a rainy day. A poorly designed parking lot will have many puddles where a well-designed one will channel the water away seamlessly. Before construction, the builder or engineer also must consider the actual makeup of material needed for unique or harsh environments. Sidewalks have angles and drainage for the rain and textures for extra traction when walking in slippery conditions, not to mention the ease of access ramps for those who don't walk.

I really never thought much about doors until I purchased my current house. I've had several people comment on how much they love the front door. To me, it wasn't about the look, it just had a function, and it did that well. Innovative technology in the makeup of a door is often overlooked, even though we walk through them every day. Unless you are a builder or installer, you probably wouldn't know that there have been endless innovations to the makeup, features, and material used in the modern-day door. Even the windows, hinges, and locks have been made better efficient, safer, and smarter. There is nothing quite as satisfying as slamming a really solid door in a well-built door frame.

Stairs, tables, and other furniture are built to be functional, yet I'm sure we have all seen homes with each of those installed or used uniquely and creatively. The beauty of some is in its space-saving structure. Others stand out because of hidden storage features like drawers and closet-type spaces. Others fold or slide away to create more floor area. There is even an entire industry dedicated to creative ways to organize and store your clothes. Not to mention the many that have a multi-function build in like the fold-out sofa sleeper, trundle bed, murphy bed, or murphy table. There are coffee tables that lift up to function as a desk. There are even multi-function living cubes that have everything from a bed, closet space, entertainment center, and even a table and chairs built into something that only takes up an eight-foot by five-foot space.

I tend to geek out as my mind tears apart these things to see how they work. It's easy to see the creativity in everyday things when you can see the working parts performing their functions. You can see how much engineering goes into all the surrounding things. You can view them from both the user's and designer's points of view. Not only do you see how a desk was engineered as you are putting it together, but you also can see the engineering that went into how it was packaged for shipping. There is a certain beauty in seeing how something is designed, how that is then broken down and packaged for shipping, then the design for the reassembly procedure. It's a man-made symbiosis living in a build, disassembly, and reassembly circle of life ecosystem.

I have been riding, racing, and working on motorcycles most of my life. Pretty much every motorcycle I've owned was made in Japan, so you need metric wrenches to work on it. The beautiful thing is that almost every major bolt is either 8, 10, or 12mm. Someone took a little creativity and made it possible for me to do most of the work on my bike with only 3 wrenches. If you spend any time working on something like that, you totally appreciate the extra thought that goes into small details that minimize the effort for the end-user.

Expressiveness and creativity are a big part of the action sports world. You see the same type of creative expression in freestyle motocross, the different disciplines of skateboarding, BMX, scooters, skates, skis, snowboards, or parkour. It could be on land, on water, snow, ice, or air. Every stunt or move is planned and perfected long before it is performed, but each person expresses themselves with their own unique twist on the stunt performed. The same stunt can look totally different performed by different people. Each person takes the base move and tweaks it just a bit to make it unique. For the most part, it is an unwritten rule; if you are the first person to do the stunt, you can name it. That move becomes whatever you call it, no matter who performs it after you do.

As a creative person, I tend to put my own style spin on everyday objects around me. The creative expression is sometimes for show, but often it's just for my own personal preference. That goes beyond the physical world into the digital world as well. I've always said that "I shouldn't have to fit the technology; the technology should fit me." I want to customize everything to work and look the way I want. Just like someone picks a case for their phone that best suits their style or need, I not only want to do that, but I also want to give my cell phone a unique look on the inside. I add customized launchers that provide me particular functionality and look beyond the stock OS from the factory. I want that perfect wallpaper and the perfect mix of individual icons per app. It's not something that is seen or appreciated by others but increases my workflow and relaxes my mindset as I use the device.

Long before we were able to change the look of our phones, I was part of the large community that jailbroke or rooted our phones. Jailbreaking or Rooting a phone removes software limitations imposed by the manufacturer. For example, I modded an iPhone very early on so it could record video. This was way before Apple released the ability for video on a future model. Being creative in that sense wasn't to show off or evoke an emotion in others. It was to see if I could advance the device's performance beyond what the factory intended … and to be able to record video with my phone. I ended up evoking an emotion in myself, pride for being able to make a phone do something very few others could at that time.

My expression of machine modification also goes beyond just phones. Like most tech-savvy people, I did every mod and upgrade to pretty much every computer I've ever owned. Again, it wasn't to show off my skills but to customize a tool I worked with every day. It was a part of my studio and was used for everything from making music to sending emails. My creativity in those things was function-driven primarily to streamline my workflow, and that again evoked joy.

That mentality goes into my DJ equipment as well. I customized my DJ software and hardware. I took older units intended to play music off a disc or attached thumb drives and customized them to work directly with the DJ software on my laptop. A lot of the MIDI map editing is built into the software now, but 10 or 15 years ago, it was many extra steps to accomplish a straightforward task. To me, it was worth it just to see if I could do it and also to get what I want.

The subtle creativity in everyday things is all around us. It plays itself out without us giving it a second thought. Each of us sees what we want in the world around us. Some look at an object and just see it for what it is. Others look at that object and see how it can be improved or what else it can be used for. They appreciate what amazing things the designer or engineer put into it from step one, and they also see more possibilities. They may never do or say their ideas, but they can't help but think, "If the engineer just did this, it would have changed everything." I'm guessing that's why many people become engineers, to fix everything they see wrong.

Imagine seeing the world like that. Everything you come across, you tear it apart and try to understand its current function and how it could be better. Most of the time, how something is built doesn't always come down to common sense uses. It comes down to making it a certain way that just saves the company money. The ability to figure out how to save money building that product was a creative journey in itself. Many final products result from a person saying several times, "That is great, but can you make it cost less" There are people whose whole job is to help a company save money. That is a tremendous skill that often requires a lot of creativity, but most people don't see that step or even think about what it takes to get a product to the final shippable stage.

The funny thing is, if you reverse the observation process, you start to see how everything around you was made and or improved. If you are old enough, you remember someone's creativity removed the pull tab on a can of soda and made it a pop-top. You've watched things go from corded to cordless. Tiny pocket LED flashlights now put out as much light as baseball bat size lights once did. Think about all the things that used to require cash or you to physically go somewhere. Now with a phone, you can pay your bills, feed parking meters, call for a ride somewhere, order food, deposit a check, digitize your rewards cards, manage a shopping list, buy and trade stocks without a broker and you get the point.

Each of these things was the result of someone's mind seeing what most others couldn't. They see the world through creative lenses that make the everyday inanimate objects around them come to life. There is beautiful creativity in all the things of nature and of man. If you creatively look at the world around you, the ugly or boring can be beautiful and inspiring. Stop and look at the next five objects you touch. Think about how it was made to be used and think if you used it for something other than it was intended. Look at man-made objects outside and think about what went into them from the planning stage to completion. Look at nature and everything from the tiny to the enormous work together from birth to death. Look at your fellow humans; see them with the depth of backstory they deserve. See how they have grown and how they fulfill a need to those around them. To see their "everyday" yet miraculous life-changing actions.

Try to see the world without your opinion getting in the way. Try to perceive it from the point of view that you don't know what will come next. Remember when everything was new to you and before your imagination was desensitized by the repetition of life. You are in charge of how you see the world around you and the people in it. Yes, there is a lot of ugly in both the world and in people, but there is also a lot of humble, creative beauty expressed in the said and the unsaid. Finally, stop and think about what you add to all of this. More importantly, think about what you can add to all of this. As long as you are alive, you can be a creative, positive addition to the world. You can continue creative beauty in everything and everyone you touch, not to mention yourself. It all begins by opening your eyes and seeing past what you already know.

Chapter 15
My Final Thoughts

Some people say when you hit tough times, the first thing that gets eliminated is creativity. I believe it is such an integrated part of everyday life no matter how hard times get; it's still there, just not recognized for its importance. Living through 2020 has shown me that being creative, expressive, and imaginative during tough times makes the unfamiliar feel normal. It gives an inner balance that is hard to define. This was one of the most unique times anyone could ever experience. Life as we knew it just stopped for most or drastically changed for others. It was like a ship on a calm sea one moment, then totally engulfed by a massive storm the next. It teaches us that sometimes you have to enter the eye of the storm to understand what you are going through and that knowledge will give you the confidence to weather the next one. The storm will give you clarity between something you are passionate about and something that just interests you. There is one fundamental difference between an interest and a passion. An interest will require you to be disciplined in its perfection, where a passion is its own discipline. You can't turn it off, you can't deny it, and you certainly can't ignore it forever. No matter how far you run or how many walls you build, that passion will always find you because it has been inside you all along. You can choose to go a different path in life, but at some point, you will be face to face with it again. Face your fears and at least accept your creative side as being normal and beneficial.

In chapter one, I talk about my "why" and "how" of this book. Creativity has its own why and how questions as well. The "why" question is answered by the passion that drives you. The "how" is just the form you choose to express your creativity. My "why" for this book was telling the story of my creative journey so it might encourage others to embrace theirs. My "how" is every word on every page of this book. At least it is; for now, when the book is finished, I'll move on to something else. The important thing is I continually get to be creative. I get to challenge myself and grow my mind through the journey. It isn't something someone can take away or something that goes away. I can only choose to give it away, attempt to ignore it, or replace it temporarily with a short-term interest. Even the sidetrack of a new interest is good for your creativity. You are giving your mind something new to learn, and that increases your brain's strength and broadens the field of your creativity. Its end result is pure positive growth in all dimensions. Whatever you do, don't fight or force your brain into being creative. As long as you accept it and nurture it, your brain will find a path to creativity. It will do the work necessary because it already wants to learn and create, even without the conscious mind's permission.

Have you ever seen one of the tests where the spelling of each word in a sentence is scrambled, but you're still able to read it? Example: Yuo cna porbalby raed tihs esaliy desptie teh msispeillgns

One way to look at this is that your brain is anticipating or predicting what words would logically come next to form a complete, coherent sentence. I look at it as your brain is continually creating from things it has seen before. If someone says to draw a tree, what you're probably going to do is draw something that resembles many different trees you have seen in your life all put together into one. When looking at a sentence, like the one above, where the letters are scrambled, if the first and last letter of each word is correct, your mind will fill in the gaps with pictures of what it has seen before. With the creative brain, the words are also seen as pictures. Creativity draws from the seen and the unseen. It continually processes the world around you, even on a subconscious level. Your brain will be creative without your permission, so why not lean into it and go along and enjoy the ride.

Most of the time, your mind plays a more significant part in you arriving at your goals than your actions do. Many people imagine doing something grand, but they never get started because they rarely believe they can. Before you do something, you must imagine yourself doing it, and before you imagine it, you have to, at least, believe you can imagine it. Your imagination makes it possible for you to believe you can do it, and that will give you the confidence to try over and over. You have to give yourself unconditional permission to believe in yourself even if no one else does. The simple act of imagining or "visualizing" yourself doing something will improve your skills and abilities almost as much as repeating the physical act does. 1992 Olympic Gold medalist Sally Gunnell says that winning is 70% in the mind. Besides daily practices, she would visualize herself running the 400-meter hurdles over and over in her mind. She visualized herself pushing stronger and stronger all the way to the finish line. The following year at the 92 Olympics, she won gold.

I've written before how creativity is often an inward journey that produces an outward result. Sometimes it's a tangible artwork, sometimes it's measured in happiness or peace of mind. Either way, it's your journey for your reasons. No one can take it from you, and even though you can learn from the journey of others, you will ultimately reap the most from your own pilgrimage. Just like you have gained and grown from seeing where others have traveled, others will grow from the overflow of what you have gained along the way. The complexity of taking that journey is the crazy part. Many times, it took me feeling completely safe on the outside before I could take a step, yet other times the creativity came from sheer self-defense from some sort of mental or emotional attack. I'm sure many of those attacks were from my own inner voice doing the tearing down. Other times, it only took a spark from someone on the outside to power that inner light. Sometimes we try to seek someone to blame for where we are, but often that's just the process of life. We are all the sum of our own choices, so choose to not quit and press forward. You might be able to grow a more beautiful flower if you learn the hard way how to keep the weeds from growing around it.

The creative act of writing helps me have access to my own words and thoughts that were previously blocked by the noise of the world. I sometimes let life overshadow my own advice and logic. At the top of Maslow's hierarchy, you will find self-actualization, also known as realizing your full potential. Below that is esteem or respect for yourself and others. Next down the hierarchy is relationships or the sense of belonging and love. Then you will find safety, security, and stability. At the very bottom are the basics like food, water, and shelter. The creative mind doesn't see a bottom-up or top-down view. Each of them is on an even plane with creativity in front of them. Creativity is the only thing that can help each of those grow. It enables you to understand that reaching your full potential is more important than just reaching your goals.

Here is where I think it all comes together. You can approach life from any angle you want. You can set any destination you wish. You can even plan out every step in your journey, but more often than not, along that journey, life happens. As much as I would like life to be predictable, it just isn't, but that doesn't mean the unforeseen things weren't meant to be. If you know me at all, you know my faith is the most important thing to me. I usually don't say too much about it unless someone asks because I can't prove to you what I believe any more than you can prove to me what you believe. I live my life by my beliefs, and I will never let anyone bully me because they think I'm wrong. I can't make your choices for you anymore than you can make mine for me. We just have to accept that we are not accountable for another's actions, but we are absolutely for our own. My choice is a loving God who is kind, gentle, and always there for us. It was once said that "Faith can move mountains but don't be surprised if God hands you a shovel." The outcome may be undetermined or unpredictable, but your actions along the way are always one choice at a time. You can't start from yesterday, just from today, right where you are at this point. No one knows the outcome for sure, but you can say with some certainty where your next step will be so, be where your feet are. Start from there with your basics like your stability, relationships, self-respect, and the realization that you are you, and there is nothing wrong with that. Just don't be afraid to ask yourself, "What can the best me be"?

I do believe that anything is possible. You absolutely can achieve anything you set your mind to. Just know before you start, there is some serious personal math involved. You can only have so much on your plate at once. You can create the next masterpiece, but you will have to remove something (or things) from your plate. Removing them may be temporary or permanent; either way, this will not only affect you but also those close to you, those who rely on you. That is why the personal math is so serious; you may have to make the painful choice to remove something that you actually want in order to achieve your dream. For most artists, the things that get removed come from the middle of Maslow's hierarchy. The first things to go are usually stability, relationships, and the concern for what others think of you. Those are typically replaced by the urgency to create no matter the time, place, or resources. Relationships and community are replaced with solitude and endless inner monologue. Finally, the two-way street of caring what others think of you and what you are doing is blocked off as needed. It is the duality of a tunnel vision and omni-focus mentality. The Maslow Hierarchy is rearranged to fit your daily creative needs. It doesn't matter if you suffer or do without, as long as your creativity is satisfied. You may have to make extraordinary sacrifices to have a story worth telling in the future.

For some people, deciding to remove things from the "normal life" is easy. They (at least for now) don't see the "normal life" as something they desire at all. I once had a friend ask me, "Don't you want a normal job and family so people will respect you?" I remember laughing a little at how he seemed to put the opinion of others above what he wanted. The "normal" job and family may have been what he actually wanted, but the "why" value he expressed to me seemed fake or imaginary. Everyone has a dream or idea of how they want their life to be, and each person should have the freedom to make whatever choices they want. I just never understood how the opinion of someone that isn't even in your daily life changes your Maslow's hierarchy pyramid. I know how hard it is to look past the expectations of the world around you and the people closest to you. There is a tangible illusion of outward opinion we as humans tend to hang our hats on. It's hard to ignore because there is a sort of frustrated resentment when others find a difference between what they expect us to be and who we actually are. We sometimes see their opinion as an essential building block for our lives instead of what it is, just a passing cloud.

Without knowing it, I have been trying to create a life that I don't need to take a vacation from. Just like real vacations, that kind of life comes with a high price many are not willing to pay. Will Smith once said, "99% of people are not willing to do what it takes to make their dreams come true." He was talking about self-discipline and how it is a fundamental building block to success. You can't have your cake and eat it too, so you have to first decide what you want and what you are willing to give up to achieve that. It took a pandemic lockdown for me to realize how important the life and career I built are to me. I could easily go out and get a job that is called essential and has a predictable income, but I know I will never be happy there. In that place, I will always be working for the weekend or the next day off. My time away from what I do should not be the motivating factor for me to do that better at that job. Money is essential, but it shouldn't be what drives me either. I said this in an earlier chapter: *money can't make you happy; it can only entertain you temporarily.*

For me, it took losing some of that steady, reliable income to find some peace of mind. I took a lot of money and exchanged it for less money and a pile of things that are so much better for me.

You can't take money out of the equation, but you can reduce the amount you need. Being in debt will significantly reduce what you can invest in your dreams. This not only means money but also time and energy. To achieve that goal, you may have to be willing to possibly take many shiny new things of life off your plate. Again, you can have what you want, but you must first decide what you may have to do without and how long you are willing to do without it. Among those choices could be more than material things or creature comforts; it could be other people. Everything we do in life affects those around us. If we decide to set an importance to living a very minimalist life to chase our passion, who in your life will that impact? If they are willing to make the sacrifices also, that is amazing. To have a partner who supports the decision to change your Maslow's hierarchy is priceless. Unfortunately for most, that decision can cost them their current relationship or future ones. You have to ask yourself, is that something I am willing to let go of or put off until far in the future? It is always your decision to make, but diving in without thinking about it is a fool's errand. I don't want what I'm saying to deter you from your goals, but I believe there are some required equations you need to calculate if you hope to get a positive outcome. You have to take full responsibility for any choices you make along the way. It's like standing on train tracks when a train is speeding your way. You can decide to stay on the tracks or decide to get off the tracks but not making a decision still leaves you on the tracks. If your decision is to make no decision, the time will come when the train will leave a lasting impact that could cost you everything in the end.

One of the other things I believe is fundamental to obtaining your final goal is perseverance. I usually tell people whatever time frame you think something will take, give yourself four times that amount. I feel that some things took so long they feel like a completely different lifetime than what I am living now. My younger years of drawing and art seem more like something I have watched or read instead of living. I was a totally different person back then than I am now. Even though other chapters in this book cover individual time periods in my life, each one seems like its own separate lifetime. I don't know if that is the same for everyone, but I know that when you have a few years under your belt, you will be amazed at how life changes you and your point of view. You will not be the same person in your 30s that you are in your 20s. In 1957, Allen Saunders wrote, "Life is what happens to us while we are making other plans." Life keeps going no matter where we are in our individual journey. It's ok if you get left behind by others because you march to your own drum but never get left behind by quitting. I've always said sometimes the difference between the person who finished first and the person who finished second is the person who finished first was just the last one to quit.

Failure is always a possible outcome, but only attach it to one attempt. Failure over many attempts doesn't make you a failure. You can spend a lifetime not succeeding at something, and rarely will anyone call you a failure. You will most likely be looked up to as someone with determination and perseverance, which in itself is an achievement. I do not believe you need to suffer for your creativity; it is not a requirement. Many artists create a self-imposed form of suffering. To me, those people must not have lived much to start with. If you have been alive for any amount of time, you know you don't have to seek suffering; it will find you. The more important point to take away from that is if you do suffer, you can use it as a powerful motivation. You can use your creativity to escape your suffering. Instead of looking for new or deeper suffering, look at what you have already been through and use that. I said in an earlier chapter; the pain we each suffer is different, but pain still feels the same no matter where it hurts. Suffering is not a competition. We can create and build off the knowledge that we understand what hurting is, and that hurting is understood by everyone. Instead of using art to communicate your suffering, use it to enlighten what suffering can lead to. The Bible says, *"Suffering produces perseverance; perseverance, character and character hope."* No matter where you are on that path, know that you are on the path to hope.

When I began the journey of writing this book almost a year ago, like most people, I had no idea where the future was going. It was a strange and uncharted place we were all in. I think everyone saw it differently. I enjoyed the solitude and time to create while others went off the deep end just because sports were canceled. For some, it meant the end of a business they spent a lifetime to build. For others, it meant walking away from one job that was fun but often unstable to collect a reliable paycheck at another job that was just that, a paycheck. For me, that point felt like life let off the gas for a moment, then up shifted towards a new path all in one motion. It surprised me how much I was perfectly comfortable with this new adventure from the first night I got the epiphanies. It was like I was on a long multi-life voyage where I collected many things that I didn't need till that exact moment when the book idea was born. It doesn't matter if you believe what I believe; I just know that when I reached that moment in time, it felt like I was able to set down the past and pick up the present. I believe it was all orchestrated a long time ago, and I was just now getting to see its complex and precise pieces fighting together. That didn't make me want to aim for some far-off future; I was just able to enjoy each moment of the life I was living. Being there still feels very strange to me, but I'm more than ok with that.

When everything paused during the lockdown, I got to take a look at my entire life and see that being creative was not just something I did; it was inside me like a virus my whole life. I spoke before that a virus is not a living thing like bacteria. It's more like a set of instructions (a small collection of genetic code) that gets put into a living cell. It can't replicate without being inside a cell; it needs the cell. Those instructions then become a permanent part of our DNA.

When we catch the creative virus, it becomes a part of us forever. Because viruses don't have the same components as bacteria, they cannot be killed by antibiotics; only antiviral medications or vaccines can eliminate or reduce the severity of viral diseases. Think of the creative virus as a good set of instructions that are causing you to want to be creative. The only way to keep that virus at bay is to be creative thus my continual need to seek opportunities to create. I can't turn it off, I can only reduce the severe need to be creative … by being creative. If enough people acknowledge, accept and embrace their creative virus maybe, we might have a "creative pandemic".

I hope you have at least found something in this book that helps to clarify the world around you. I hope it shines a light on you that chases away any self-inflicted pain. I hope you can get so lost in your creations that the doubt and darkness in your life can't even find you. I hope you can better process then express how you feel about the world around you. I hope you know that creativity, expression, and imagination are your ever-present allies. I hope you see your creativity as the amazing multi-purpose tool that it is. I hope you can see the true beauty of everything around you. I hope every sound you hear becomes a song you love that causes you to dance until you feel weightless. I hope you get to play your creativity to the world until they feel that weightlessness as well. I hope your physical and digital worlds can be nurtured to live in harmony with one another. I hope you see your self-worth and no longer need lies and manipulation to help you stand. I hope you see others with love and see they love you also. I hope every word and every picture around you fills your inspirational cup till it overflows into the cups of others around the world. I hope in the midst of the good, the bad and the little, you can just have fun. I hope you also hope.

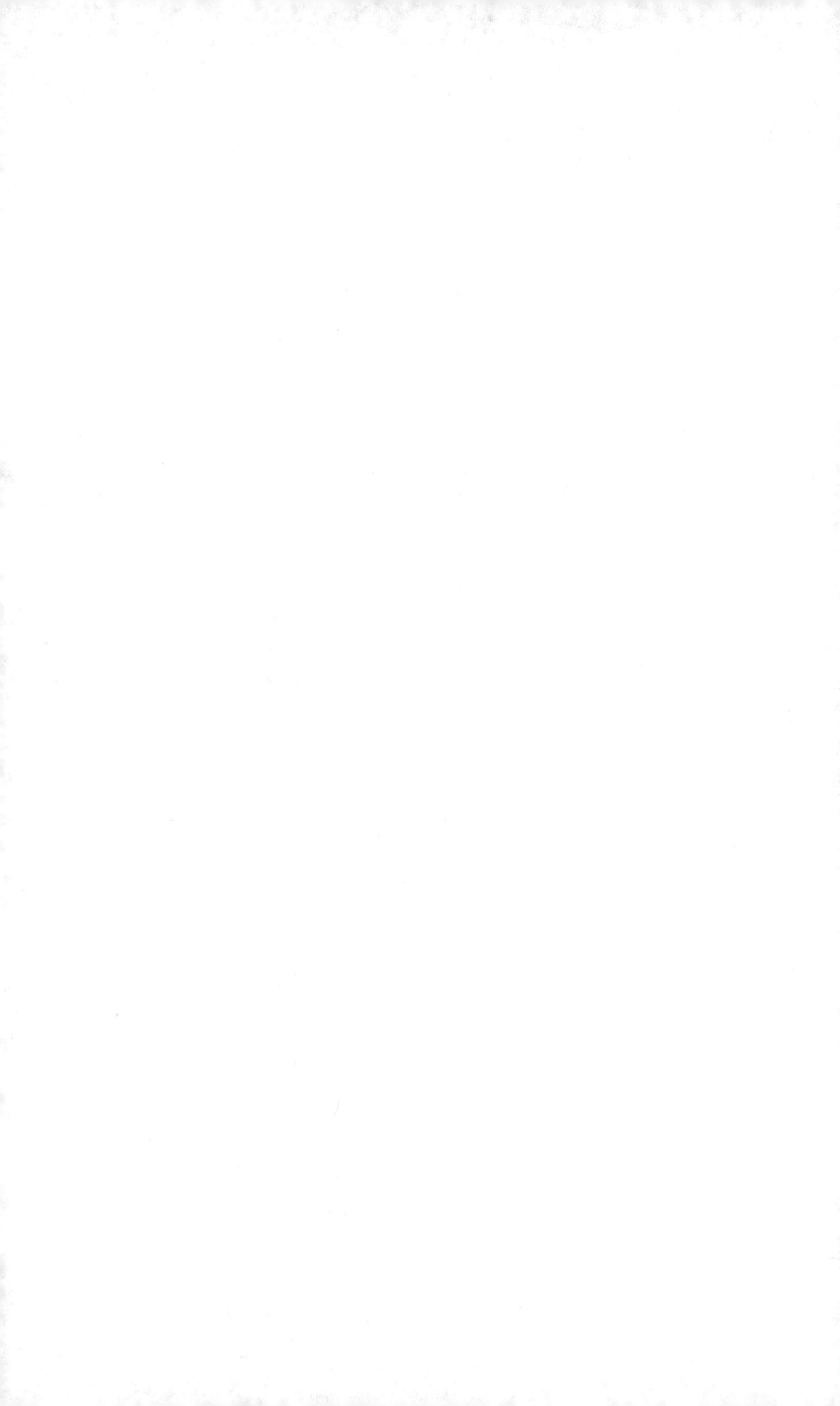